The
Apple Watch
Book

Master the most **personal computer** in your life

SCOTT MCNULTY

PEACHPIT PRESS

The Apple Watch Book:
Master the most personal computer in your life

Scott McNulty

Peachpit Press
www.peachpit.com

To report errors, please send a note to errata@peachpit.com
Peachpit Press is a division of Pearson Education

Copyright 2016 by Scott McNulty

Editors: Clifford Colby and Liz Welch
Production editor: David Van Ness
Compositors: Maureen Forys, Happenstance Type-O-Rama
Indexer: Valerie Haynes Perry
Cover Design: Aren Straiger
Interior Design: Mimi Heft

Notice of Rights

Notice of Liability

Trademarks

ISBN 13:   978-0-134-17776-2
ISBN 10:   0-134-17776-2

9 8 7 6 5 4 3 2 1
Printed and bound in the United States of America

To Glenn for being a timeless friend (see what I did there?).

Acknowledgments

You'd think the more books you write, the easier it would get. This is false. My thanks to my wife Marisa, who has managed to put up with the stress of living with a tech book author. Luckily, a lot of very smart people have helped me make this book a reality. My thanks to Cliff Colby, my stalwart editor. Liz Welch has once again managed to make my words make more sense than I could on my own. Thanks, Liz. My thanks to David Van Ness and everyone on the production team for making this book look as great as it does. And my thanks to everyone at Peachpit who helped out. I would be remiss if I didn't also thank my boss, Dan, for supporting my non-work-related activities.

Contents

Introduction

Apple Watch is a unique device, and this tech book isn't your every-day how-to guide. This book is spread out over the course of a day and follows the Peterson family as they use the Apple Watch in a variety of circumstances.

The first chapter tells you the prerequisites for using Apple Watch. It also discusses the various models of the watch and the differences between them. Finally, this chapter explores the basics of using the watch's interface.

Chapter 2 walks you through pairing the watch with your iPhone and iden-tifying the few physical buttons it has. Using Siri, launching and installing apps, and customizing watch faces are all covered in this chapter.

Chapter 3 starts off the day by covering a variety of tasks Apple Watch can help you with in the morning. From waking you up to reviewing your calendar, this chapter sets you off right.

Chapter 4 moves into the afternoon and takes your Apple Watch to work and to the store. Paying for things with your watch is covered, as is answer-ing phone calls, sending Digital Touches, and controlling presentations.

Chapter 5 completes the day by covering evening activities. Listening to music, using your watch as a remote for your Apple TV, and getting direc-tions are all explained here.

Chapter 6 offers up some easy troubleshooting tips in case you encounter any difficulties with Apple Watch.

CHAPTER 1

Introduction

Apple Watch is the most personal computer you'll have in your life. Much like any other watch, you strap it to your body, and it's designed to be worn every waking moment. However, unlike your favorite Rolex or Swatch, Apple Watch will tap you on the wrist every time you get an email. Or tell you how to get to the mall. Or quickly show you how active, or not so active, you've been so far today.

Calling Apple Watch a watch is like calling a Swiss Army knife simply a knife. Technically it's true but both do so much more. This book is designed to guide you through how to interact with your new Apple Watch, and to give you some ideas about how it can fit into your life and your day-to-day activities.

Given how different Apple Watch is from all of Apple's other devices, it makes sense that this book is structured a little differently as well. Instead of having a list of instructions, this book is organized around a typical day in the life of a typical Apple Watch–loving family. The fictional family in question is the Petersons: Bob and Mary with their teenage daughter Billie and tween son Aaron.

Each of the Petersons is the happy owner of an Apple Watch, though they each sport a slightly different model (more on that in the section "The Various Models"). The Petersons will be convenient stand-ins for you, the reader, as I detail how each Peterson family member uses the watch to keep in contact with each other and to get things done. This book will cover Apple Watch's built-in apps (those are the ones that Apple wrote for the watch and that are available right out of the box) as well as highlight some of the best third-party apps currently available for the watch.

Apple enjoys a rich ecosystem of passionate developers who create amazing apps to run on these amazing devices. There are thousands of Apple Watch apps, with more becoming available every day. Don't limit yourself to the apps I recommend in this book; look around the App Store (covered in the next chapter) and see what's there. If you can think of it, chances are there's at least one Apple Watch app available to do it. For example, I'm an avid pen-and-paper role-playing game player, and I (half-jokingly) looked for dice-rolling apps for the watch. There are at least five currently available.

Apple Watch Prerequisites

Before you run out and buy yourself an Apple Watch, you need to know a little secret about the watch: all of its functionality works only when it is paired with an iPhone (other smartphone types, like Android, are not supported by Apple Watch). And not just any iPhones will do! Make sure you have an iPhone 5 or later or you'll be disappointed when you can't pair your watch with your phone (more on the pairing process in the next chapter, "The Day of Arrival").

▶ **NOTE** Your Apple Watch pairs wirelessly to your iPhone using Bluetooth. When your iPhone is out of range or powered down, your Apple Watch doesn't stop working altogether. You can still use it to tell the time, to set alarms, as a stopwatch, to play music from locally synced playlists (see the "Music" section in Chapter 5, "Evening"), to use the Workout app, to display photos (see the "Photos" section in Chapter 5), and to use Apple Pay to purchase things from participating retailers (see the section "Apple Pay" in Chapter 4, "Afternoon").

If you're the happy owner of an iPhone 5 or later, you're one step closer to being Apple Watch ready. The next step is making sure you have the right version of iOS (the software that powers your iPhone). You have to have at least iOS 8.2 in order to pair your Apple Watch. If you have the right level of iOS, you'll find an Apple Watch app on your iPhone (**Figure 1.1**).

Figure 1.1 The Apple Watch app is only available on compatible iPhones.

You can also check the version of iOS directly on your iPhone through the Settings app. Your iOS version is displayed in the Version section of the General Settings. Anything above 8.2 means you can pair an Apple Watch with your iPhone. Find the version of iOS on your phone by

1. Tapping the Settings icon (**Figure 1.2**)

Figure 1.2 The Settings app allows access to a variety of iPhone settings.

2. Tapping General > About

3. Scrolling until you see the Version section (**Figure 1.3**)

4. Pressing the Home button to return to your iPhone's app list

Once you've verified that you have the correct iPhone and the proper version of iOS, there's nothing stopping you from buying yourself an Apple Watch. But which one suits your needs?

Figure 1.3 Apple
Watch requires
iOS 8.2 or later.

Name	Scott McNulty's iPhone >
Network	AT&T
Songs	6
Videos	4
Photos	374
Applications	82
Capacity	113 GB
Available	96.5 GB
Version	8.3 (12F70)

The Various Models

You can choose from three different kinds of Apple Watch: Apple Watch Sport, Apple Watch, and Apple Watch Edition. Each comes in two sizes, accounting for the different sizes of people's wrists: 38mm or 42mm. (The 38MM watch is 33.3mm wide whereas the 42MM model is 35.9mm wide. They are both 10.5mm deep.) Additionally, Apple has created a number of bands that can be easily swapped (so why not buy several bands?).

Oddly enough, although the materials that make up each kind of Apple Watch differ (more on that in a moment), the internals are all the same. Each Apple Watch has the following features:

- Bluetooth
- An organic light-emitting diode (OLED) touchscreen display
- A number of sensors, including a heart rate monitor, ambient light, a gyroscope, and an accelerometer
- Identical battery life of about 18 hours (according to Apple)
- 8 GB of total storage

Why are there three different types of Apple Watch when they all have the same features? Fashion! Each version of the Apple Watch is created from different materials and comes in at different price points (see **Table 1.1**).

APPLE WATCH SPORT

Available in silver or "space gray," this is the most affordable entry in the Apple Watch line (starting at $349). It has an Ion-X glass display, which is scratch resistant and hard to shatter. This model also comes with a fluoroelastomer (that's a special rubber) band designed to resist absorbing sweat. This model is light and durable, and it's designed for people on a budget or who want to work out with their Apple Watch.

APPLE WATCH

Also available in silver or space gray, Apple Watch has a stainless steel case and a sapphire crystal display. The display is very tough, but it's brittle when compared to the Ion-X glass display, so if you often bang your watch face into things you might want to save some money (and heartache) and stick with an Apple Watch Sport. Apple Watch can be purchased, starting at $549, with a variety of band combinations. This watch is geared toward people looking for a slightly higher-end finish.

APPLE WATCH EDITION

Starting at $10,000, the Apple Watch Edition isn't for everyone. The cases are solid gold (18-karat yellow or rose gold to be precise). The display is the same sapphire crystal as you'll find in Apple Watch, though I doubt many people will be working out while wearing an Apple Watch Edition. Since this is the very high end of the line, it comes in a special box that doubles as a charger (a nice touch). This is the watch for people who can afford luxury watches or for those folks who love gold.

Given the two sizes, as well as the wide variety of materials and bands, you'll probably want to pay a visit to your local Apple Store and see the Apple Watches in person. Try a few on and get an idea of which size works best on your wrist.

If you're not close to an Apple Store. you can still determine which size is for you by using the Apple Store app on your iPhone:

1. Tap the Apple Store icon to launch the app.

2. Tap Shop > Apple Watch to go to the Apple Watch section of the store.

3. Tap on any of the Apple Watch models and then tap the Buy Now button in the top-right corner of the screen (**Figure 1.4**).

Figure 1.4 The Apple Watch section of the Apple Store app.

THE APPLE WATCH BOOK

4. Swipe right to left to cycle through the watches. Tap "Compare case sizes" to see the various cases in their actual size (**Figure 1.5**).

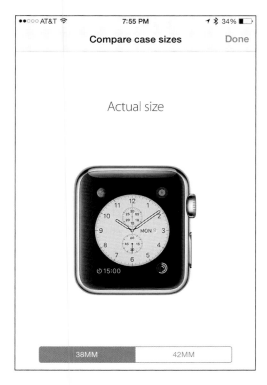

Figure 1.5 Get a sense for the Apple Watch size using the Apple Store sizing tool.

5. Hold your iPhone against your wrist and toggle between 38MM and 42MM to see which works best for you.

Apple Watch Basics

The Petersons have all ordered their Apple Watches and they're excited to set them up. However, some Apple Watch–specific terms are bound to pop up that deserve our attention first. Some of the terms will be familiar to you if you're an iPhone user, but Apple Watch adds some unique interactions to the mix:

Tap: Much as you tap something on an iPhone or iPad, you tap things on the Apple Watch display with your finger (some features are activated by a two-finger tap). This includes buttons (like tapping in your password) or icons (to launch an app).

Force touch: Force touch is the newest interaction available on the watch. You're used to tapping on buttons on touchscreens, but you force touch by thinking of the display itself as a button. Tap, and then apply some more pressure to the display and you've just force touched. This interaction is used in many sections of Apple Watch to bring up secondary menus.

Swipe: Swiping involves pressing your finger against the Apple Watch display and dragging it up, down, left, or right. Swiping up is dragging your finger up, and so on. This is a major interaction method for the watch.

Drag: To move items around on your Apple Watch (like, for example, app icons on the Home screen), press on the item and drag your finger across the display to the where you'd like the item to be. Once you lift your finger, you'll see that the item has been dragged into its new position. You can also use the drag gesture to navigate around certain screens; I'll cover that whenever doing so is an option.

Pressing: The Apple Watch sports two physical buttons: the Digital Crown and the Side button. *Pressing* is the term that will be used when you need to interact with either of these buttons.

Scrolling: Neither variant of the Apple Watch display is particularly large, so you're going to end up scrolling from time to time. You can do this either by swiping up and down with your finger or by turning the Digital Crown. I recommend using the Digital Crown as often as possible for scrolling since it is a much smoother experience.

Zooming: Another concession to the fact that these watch displays aren't that big is zooming. Turning the Digital Crown on certain screens (like the Apps screen) will zoom in or out.

Haptic feedback: All of the previously listed interactions are about you touching Apple Watch, but Apple Watch can also touch you, in a way. It includes something called a Taptic Engine, which allows it to tap you on the wrist when you get a notification (this is known as "haptics"). Every time you get a notification on your watch, you'll feel a tap on your wrist. You can also send taps to your other Apple Watch–using friends (see the "Digital Touch" section in Chapter 4) or send them your heartbeat, which will display on the watch and tap in time with your heart on their wrists (also covered in the "Digital Touch" section).

The various bits of interface on the Apple Watch also have their own vocabulary, which will be used throughout the book:

Notifications: Much like on your iPhone, apps can display alerts on your Apple Watch. These alerts are called *notifications* and they're designed to give you a brief piece of information (you have a new email) and give you some actions that you can take (reply, delete, and so on). The notification settings on your iPhone dictate which apps can send your Apple Watch notifications. You can toggle these settings on and off in the Apple Watch app on your iPhone (more about dealing with notifications in the next chapter).

Apps: A number of apps are available for installation on your Apple Watch. These apps can do everything from tracking your run to allowing you to search your notes in Evernote. Generally, these apps are companion apps for its iPhone parent app. App management, including installation, organizing, and deleting, happens through the Apple Watch app on your iPhone.

Glances: Glances are a facet of Apple Watch apps. They provide a quick snippet of information that you can consume in a glance, just by swiping up when you're on the watch face. Glances show you the amount of battery left on your Apple Watch, your appointments, and more. Glances can also include some limited functionality. For example, the Remote glance allows you to start and stop the music player. Glances can be reordered, toggled on and off, and disabled entirely from the iPhone Apple Watch app.

CHAPTER 2

The Day of Arrival

In this chapter the Petersons' new Apple Watches arrive and are paired with their iPhones. This chapter covers what's included with each Apple Watch as well as how to charge the device, swap out bands, tell the time, and even customize the watch face.

Touring the Watch

The Petersons have all ordered Apple Watches. Bob is a higher end watch kinda guy, so he sprang for the Apple Watch. Mary is training for a marathon, and the kids don't need fancy watches, so they all went with the Apple Watch Sport (with different color bands).

Tearing open the Apple Watch boxes reveals the Apple Watch and a few other things:

- A Quick Tips Guide (though this book is far better, so bully to you for buying it).
- The band (whichever band the purchaser opted for). The Sports band comes with pieces to make it fit your wrist. The band half with the holes is labeled S for Small or M/L for Medium/Large wrists.
- A 6-foot-long magnetic charger cable (**Figure 2.1**) and a USB power adapter to plug the cable into (for more about charging your Apple Watch, see "Charging" later in this chapter).

Figure 2.1 The charger for your Apple Watch has a nice long cord.

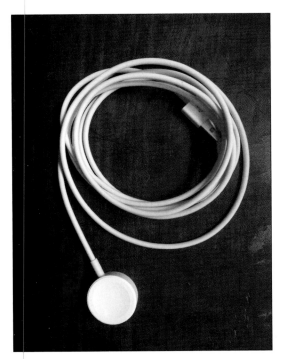

That covers the contents of the Apple Watch Sport and the Apple Watch. If you opted for the Apple Watch Edition, you'll find a couple more things:

- A magnetic charging case (in addition to the charging cable).

- A Lightning-to-USB cable. Plug the Lightning end into the case and the USB end into the USB power adapter to make the charging case charge.

As I mentioned in Chapter 1, "Introduction," all Apple Watches have the same features, no matter which type you buy. They also all have the same physical buttons (**Figure 2.2**).

Figure 2.2 Apple Watch has only two physical buttons: the Digital Crown and the Side button.

The first thing Mary notices about her Apple Watch is the screen. It takes up almost the entire front of the case and is the surface used most when interacting with the watch. To the right of the screen are Apple Watch's two physical buttons:

- **The Digital Crown:** The idea of a crown may be familiar to you if you're used to wearing watches that require winding. It's the little button on the side of a traditional watch that you spin to wind and set the watch. On Apple Watch the time doesn't need to be manually set, but you spin the Digital Crown to scroll through notifications, to zoom in and out of the Apps list, and to generally adjust your view. It's also a button that can be pressed. Press it once to go to Apple Watch's Home screen (see the section "Apps" later in this chapter), double-click it to return to the last used app, and press and hold to activate Siri (see the "Siri" section later in this chapter for more information).

- **The Side button:** Directly below the Digital Crown is the imaginatively named Side button. Press it once to show or hide the Friends screen (see the section "Friends" in Chapter 4, "Afternoon"). Double-clicking brings up Apple Pay (see the "Apple Pay" section in Chapter 4). Press and hold to turn on Apple Watch when it's off. When it's on, you can press and hold the Side button until the watch turns off, tap on one of the options that appears to lock the watch (see the section "Locking" later in this chapter, or use Power Reserve (see the "Power Reserve" section of Chapter 5, "Evening") (**Figure 2.3**).

Figure 2.3 Holding in the Side button allows you to turn off your Apple Watch, among other options.

Flip Apple Watch over and you'll see

- **The two band release buttons:** Press one of these buttons and you can slide a band section off your watch. You can then replace it by sliding another Apple Watch band in its place until you hear the button lock.

- **The heart rate sensor:** Almost the entire back of the watch is devoted to the heart rate sensor. In order for the sensor to work best, you have to make sure that you tighten the band on your wrist securely. If the watch back doesn't contact your skin firmly the heart sensor won't work well (and Apple Watch will keep asking you for a password, but more on that in a moment). The heart sensor uses a combination of infrared and green LED lights to measure your heart rate using *photoplethysmography*—basically, by measuring light absorption Apple Watch determines your heart rate. It does this automatically every 10 minutes, when possible.

- **Speaker and microphone:** You'll see two parallel lines and a small hole on one side of the watch's back. The hole is the microphone that makes it possible for your Apple Watch to hear what you're saying. The parallel lines are a tiny speaker that produces alert sounds. Using these two in combination allows you to talk on the phone on your wrist like a comic book character (see "Making Phone Calls" in Chapter 4).

▶ **NOTE** Given the wide variety of bands Apple makes for Apple Watch—a selection that will only grow larger as third-party band makers enter the market—it is impossible for this book to cover all the ways the bands clasp. Refer to your band's documentation if you're having trouble clasping it. However, all of the bands across all of the Apple Watch models are added and removed in the manner I described here.

Pairing

Now it's time to turn on your Apple Watch. Press the Side button until an Apple logo appears on the display. This means that the watch is booting up. Once it's done booting, a list of available languages is displayed. Scroll by dragging your finger on the screen. Tap the language you want, and Apple Watch tells you to open the Apple Watch app on your iPhone to begin the pairing process (**Figure 2.4**).

▶ **TIP** You'll want to have your Apple ID password handy because the pairing process will ask for it.

Figure 2.4 The first thing your Apple Watch tells you to do is pair it with an iPhone.

Grab the iPhone you want to pair your watch with and tap the Apple Watch App icon. As you do, you'll notice that your Apple Watch is displaying a unique pulsating field of dots (**Figure 2.5**).

Figure 2.5 This unique pattern is used to pair your Apple Watch with your iPhone.

Tap the Start Pairing button on the Apple Watch iPhone app and point your iPhone at your watch until it is centered (**Figure 2.6**). After only a few moments your watch is paired (**Figure 2.7**). If you've previously had a watch paired with your phone, you can restore from backup or tap "Set Up as New Apple Watch" to continue.

Figure 2.6 Using your iPhone's camera to pair with Apple Watch is an easy process.

Figure 2.7 Success! Your Apple Watch is paired, and now it can be set up as a new watch or restored from a backup.

▶ **NOTE** If this pairing process fails, there is a manual backup process. Tap "Pair manually" and the name of your Apple Watch will appear on the screen. Tap it and a code will appear on the watch. Enter that code into your iPhone and the watch will be paired.

You'll be asked which wrist you plan to wear the watch on. Tap either Left or Right (you can always change this later). Tap Agree to agree to the Terms and Conditions and then tap Agree again.

You can enter your Apple ID password by tapping Enter Password if you like (**Figure 2.8**). This will allow people to more easily find you on Digital Touch and enables Apple Pay on the watch. If you skip this step, those features will not work, though you can always enter your Apple ID later (using the Apple Watch app).

Next the Apple Watch app lets you know it is turning on Location Services for your watch (**Figure 2.9**). You can't skip this step, nor can you disable it here, but you can disable Location Services later if you don't want your watch to know where it is. Tap OK to continue.

Figure 2.8 Enter your Apple ID to enable Apple Pay.

Figure 2.9 Your watch will use your location information by default. This screen tells you how to turn that off.

Siri allows you to dictate messages to your watch, make calls, set alarms, and more (**Figure 2.10**). Once again, this is just an informational screen; you can't disable Siri from here. Tap OK to continue.

Apple would like you to automatically send diagnostics along to their Apple Watch developers whenever something not quite right happens (**Figure 2.11**). This is completely opt-in, so it is up to you. Tap Automatically Send if you don't mind sending along the information to Apple, or tap Don't Send and Apple will never hear a thing from your watch.

Next you must set a passcode for your watch (**Figure 2.12**). Tapping "Create a Passcode" will prompt you to enter a 4-digit passcode on the Apple Watch itself (**Figure 2.13**). Tapping "Add a Long Passcode" allows you to enter a passcode longer than 4 characters, though no matter what, a passcode is required to use features like Apple Pay.

Figure 2.10 Siri, Apple's voice assistant, is a big part of interacting with the Watch.

Figure 2.11 Sending diagnostics to Apple is optional.

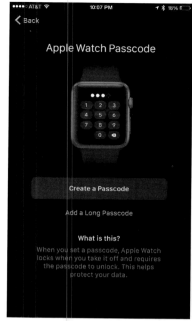

Figure 2.12 A passcode is required for Apple Watch, but you won't have to enter it often during the course of a normal day's usage.

Figure 2.13 The passcode entry screen.

Now whenever you try to use your Apple Watch when it isn't on your wrist, you'll need to enter the passcode you just set. When it is on your wrist, you have to enter the code only once; you won't be prompted to enter it again until you take the watch off.

You can set your watch to unlock whenever the paired iPhone unlocks (**Figure 2.14**). Even with this setting enabled, skin contact is required for your watch to remain unlocked.

Figure 2.14 If you tap Yes when your iPhone is unlocked, your Apple Watch will unlock too.

Your iPhone no doubt has a number of apps that have Apple Watch counterparts. You can install all of them at once by tapping Install All or select which apps you want to install on your Apple Watch by tapping Choose Later (**Figure 2.15**).

At this point, all the settings have been configured and need to be synced to your watch from the iPhone, along with all the apps if you opted to install them (**Figure 2.16**). Once it is finished syncing, the Apple Watch app will alert you (**Figure 2.17**). After the syncing process is finished, the Apple Watch displays a watch face (**Figure 2.18**).

▶ **NOTE** Complications are a good thing in the Apple Watch world. In fact, this is another term Apple has borrowed from the analog watch industry. A complication is a small piece of functionality that allows you to display specific information on the Apple Watch face.

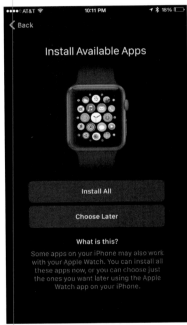

Figure 2.15 The last set of Apple Watch pairing: installing all available Watch apps from your iPhone.

Figure 2.16 The syncing process moves settings and apps onto your Apple Watch. This can take a while.

Figure 2.17 When the syncing is done, your Apple Watch is ready to go.

Figure 2.18 The default watch face with a couple of complications.

This pairing process allows your watch to communicate with your iPhone and leverage both its superior processing power and its greater network connectivity. The watch doesn't have a cell radio or GPS chip in it, so it can't wirelessly connect to a cellular data network or know its location without being paired with an iPhone.

The watch does have Wi-Fi, though it is used only to stay connected with your iPhone when they're both on the same wireless network (the iPhone tells the watch which Wi-Fi network it's on and automatically connects your watch to the same one). This extends the wireless connectivity a great deal, since normally it's a simple Bluetooth connection between the two devices, which has a range of about 200 feet.

When your watch loses its connection with the iPhone, a red phone icon with a slash appears at the top of the clock face (**Figure 2.19**).

A lot of functionality requires an active connection to an iPhone. Here's a list of things that do continue to work on your Apple Watch if your phone is out of range, turned off, or out of battery power:

- It can still tell time and do time-related things, including alarms and the stopwatch. The complications also still work.

- Activity tracking with the Activity app still tracks your exercise, steps, and more.

- You can play locally stored music and look at locally stored pictures.

- Apple Pay is available.

- Some glances, including Beats Per Minute and the battery power left on your Apple Watch, remain available.

Put It On

Now is the moment of truth. The proper bands are attached and the Peterson family is ready to don their fancy new Apple Watches. The first thing to keep in mind is that your watch should be snug on your wrist. Apple Watch is a little unsure of itself, and it needs to have constant contact with your skin in order to remain unlocked and to accurately determine your heart rate. Make sure that the Watch won't spin on your wrist; if it does, tighten the band until it remains in one place.

Once Apple Watch is on your wrist, the display will activate whenever you raise your wrist or when you tap on it or press a button. This ensures that the display is always on when you need it but that it doesn't waste battery power displaying things when you aren't even looking at your watch.

When you look at your watch for the first time on your wrist, you'll see the default watch face (Modular) and a small blue lock icon at the top of the display. That means your Apple Watch is locked. Tapping on the screen or pressing any of the buttons will bring up a keypad where you can tap your passcode to unlock the watch.

Once you've entered the passcode, you won't need to enter it again unless

- You take the watch off.
- The watch loses contact with your skin due to a loose band.
- You explicitly lock the watch.

Left or right

Traditionally if you're right-handed you wear your watch on the left wrist, and vice versa for lefties. By default Apple Watch is set up to be worn on your left wrist, with the Digital Crown on the right side of the case. However, Bob wants to wear it on his right wrist and have the Digital Crown on the left side for easier pressing.

When he puts the watch on like this without changing any settings, the interface is displayed upside down, which isn't optimal. To change orientation using the Apple Watch app on the iPhone, Bob must follow these steps:

1. Tap the app to launch it on the paired iPhone.
2. Tap General > Watch Orientation (**Figure 2.20**).
3. Tap the appropriate wrist (in this case, right) and then tap "Digital Crown on Left Side." After a moment the interface will correctly be displayed for Bob.

▶ **NOTE** This isn't just a matter of preference; Apple Watch needs to know which wrist it's being worn on so that it knows when to wake the display.

Figure 2.20 Apple Watch supports being worn on either the left or the right wrist.

Bob can also change these settings right on his Apple Watch:

1. Press the Digital Crown to go to the Home screen (**Figure 2.21**). You may need to press the Digital Crown a couple of times, depending on where you are in the Apple Watch.

Figure 2.21 The Home screen.

2. Zoom with the Digital Crown until the icons are large enough for you to see the gear icon (which is the Settings icon). You may need to drag your finger on the display to position the icon.

3. Tap the Settings icon.

4. Scroll until you see General and then tap on it (**Figure 2.22**).

Figure 2.22 You can specify General settings on your Apple Watch.

5. Tap Orientation. Here you can set the wrist and the Digital Crown to either left or right by tapping (**Figure 2.23**).

Figure 2.23 Set which wrist you're using and where the Digital Crown is right on the watch itself.

6. Press the Digital Crown to return to the Apps list, or tap Orientation to go back the General Settings list.

Siri

Siri can help you do nearly everything on your Apple Watch. The Petersons are already huge Siri fans, thanks to their iPhones, and they find Siri on Apple Watch is just as great.

There are two ways to launch Siri:

- Hold in the Digital Crown and Siri will be activated.

- Move your wrist to activate Apple Watch and say aloud, "Hey, Siri." That phrase will trigger Siri without you having to touch a thing.

Keep a couple of things in mind when using Hey, Siri:

- Make sure that the watch can hear you. Sometimes, Hey, Siri just doesn't work. Try again.

- The key to using Hey, Siri is to avoid pausing between saying "Hey, Siri" and the command you want to issue. For example, to launch the Activity app you would say, "Hey, Siri, launch Activity."

You'll know that Hey, Siri worked because after a moment the Siri screen will appear with the command she thought you said (**Figure 2.24**).

Figure 2.24 Launching apps with the power of your voice and Siri.

No matter how you launch Siri, she can do a variety of things:

- Call or text any of your contacts (see Chapter 3 for more details).

- Display sports scores (**Figure 2.25**). Scroll down to see even more information about the game, such as start time, inning/period scoring breakdowns, and more.

Figure 2.25 Siri knows all sorts of things like sports scores.

- Find out celebrity ages (**Figure 2.26**). This has settled many an argument.

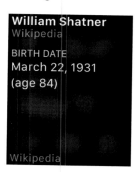

Figure 2.26 Celebrity ages and birthdays.

- Search for the nearest restaurants (**Figure 2.27**). Tapping on any of the results gives you the address, phone number, and a map that you can tap to get directions from your current location.

Figure 2.27 Nearby eateries.

- Check the weather without opening the Weather app or the glance (**Figure 2.28**). You can even check the weather in different places (**Figure 2.29**).

Figure 2.28 Check the current weather conditions near you...

Figure 2.29 ...and far away.

- Find out what movies are playing near you, with show times (**Figure 2.30**). Tapping on a movie gives you more information like length, Rotten Tomatoes rank, and which movie theater it's playing in (**Figure 2.31**). Tap on a movie theater to get directions.

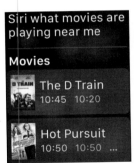

Figure 2.30 Siri can tell you what movies are playing nearby...

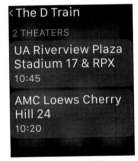

Figure 2.31 ...and what theaters they're playing in.

- You can also ask Siri general questions like, "What's the capital of Pennsylvania?" and Siri will search Wikipedia and return the answer (**Figure 2.32**). Scroll down and you'll get even more information from Wikipedia, including pictures, maps, and article text.

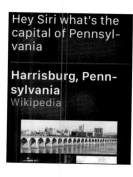

Figure 2.32 State capitals are a breeze for Siri, since she has access to Wikipedia.

Sometimes Siri won't be able to do what you ask her on your watch. For example, if you ask Siri to open a webpage or compose an email she just can't do it. She will, however, offer to use Handoff to complete the task on the paired iPhone.

Handoff, as the name suggests, hands off tasks that can't be completed on your watch to your iPhone.

Here's how to use Handoff on the paired iPhone:

1. Ask Siri to do something that she can't (like send an email). She displays the Handoff message (**Figure 2.33**).

2. Look at the lock screen on the paired iPhone and you'll see a small icon in the lower-left corner (**Figure 2.34**). Swipe up on that icon.

Figure 2.33 Handoff allows you to continue an activity started on your Apple Watch on your iPhone.

Figure 2.34 Handoff can be activated on the iPhone by tapping the icon in the lower left of the lock screen.

3. If your iPhone is locked, unlock it, and the app that Siri handed off to (in this case Safari) will open and load your request.

▶ **TIP** If you want to disable Handoff, launch the Apple Watch app, tap General, and then toggle off Enable Handoff.

As you use apps on your Apple Watch you'll notice the Handoff icon appear on your iPhone. No matter which app hands off to your iPhone, the process to use it is the same.

Remember, Siri only works when your paired iPhone is connected to a network (either the cell network or Wi-Fi). When you attempt to use Siri without your paired iPhone connected to a network, Siri will display an error message (**Figure 2.35**).

Figure 2.35 Siri requires a connection to the paired iPhone.

No Siri Connection
Neither Apple Watch nor iPhone can access Siri.

Turn off Hey, Siri

Although your Apple Watch does include voice recognition, it doesn't have enough smarts to recognize your voice and take orders only from you. Siri will respond to any voice that it hears, which can cause some accidental activations of Siri if one of your friends like to yell "Hey, Siri!" when you raise your wrist.

The potential consequences of these kinds of shenanigans are low. However, if you don't want this to happen you easily can disable Hey, Siri:

1. On your Apple Watch press the Digital Crown until you're on the Home screen. Tap the Settings app icon (**Figure 2.36**).

Figure 2.36 The Settings icon looks like a gear.

2. Tap General and scroll down until you see Siri.

3. Tap Siri. Tap Hey, Siri to toggle this setting off (**Figure 2.37**). Tap again to toggle it back on.

Figure 2.37 Hey Siri can be turned on and off.

Apps

Apple Watch supports a number of apps, so let's talk about how to launch apps, install apps, arrange your apps, and remove apps from your watch.

Launching apps

Mary is eager to jump into some Apple Watch apps, but she opted not to install any apps when pairing her iPhone with her watch (see "Pairing"). That's okay, because Apple Watch comes with a variety of stock apps, which all live on the Home screen (**Figure 2.38**). When you install new apps on your watch (see the next section), their icons will also appear on the Home screen.

Figure 2.38 The Home screen is where you access both stock and third-party apps on your watch.

Press the Digital Crown to get to the Home screen. Drag your finger on the display to pan around the icons, and find the app you're after. You can zoom in and out by turning the Digital Crown.

Tap the icon of the app you want and the app will launch. Press the Digital Crown to return to the Home screen.

If you know the name of the app you want to launch, here's an easy way to launch apps: use your voice. Press the Digital Crown in to activate Siri. Say "Open" and then the name of an app installed on your watch. Siri will display what she thought you said and then attempt to open the app. If Siri can't find the app, she'll display an error message.

Installing apps

Apple Watch apps are companions to their iPhone counterparts. Any additional apps for your watch require that an app be installed on the paired iPhone first. This means you can't install apps directly from your watch, which is why there isn't an App Store icon on your watch.

Although there isn't an App Store on your watch, there *is* a Watch App Store that lists all the currently available Apple Watch apps. To get to it:

1. Launch the Apple Watch app on your paired iPhone.

2. Tap the Featured icon on the bottom of the app and the featured Apple Watch apps will be displayed (**Figure 2.39**). Much like the App Store for iPhone/iPad apps, you tap an app icon to see more details (**Figure 2.40**). Screen shots, reviews, and related apps are all available here.

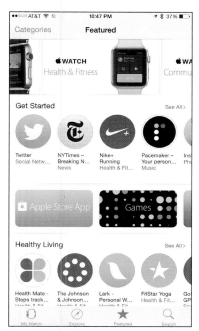

Figure 2.39 The Watch App Store is available via the iPhone Apple Watch app.

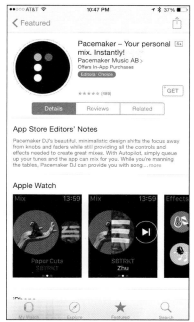

Figure 2.40 An Apple Watch App Store entry has everything you would expect: reviews, screen shots, descriptions, and price (where appropriate).

3. Tap the Get or Price button to get the app for your watch. If the app is free, the Get button will transform into an Install button. If this is a paid app, you'll need to enter your Apple ID and confirm your purchase.

4. Tap Install and the app is installed on your iPhone and then onto the watch.

You can also search the App Store if you don't see what you're looking for in the Featured section. Tap the Search icon at the bottom of the Apple Watch app (see **Figure 2.39**) and enter a search term. Any apps that meet your search criteria are displayed, and you can install them using the same directions.

▶ **TIP** When you're in the Featured section there's a Categories button in the upper-left section. Tap on this to see the full list of watch app categories. Tap on a category to see the featured apps in that category or, in the case of games, a list of subcategories, each with their own featured pages.

You probably already have some apps on your iPhone that have Apple Watch counterparts. To have them install on your watch, just launch the Apple Watch app, go to the My Watch section, and scroll down until you see the list of third-party apps (**Figure 2.41**). Tap on the app you want to show up on your watch and toggle on "Show App on Apple Watch." The app will start installing and after a few moments it'll be on your watch (**Figure 2.42**).

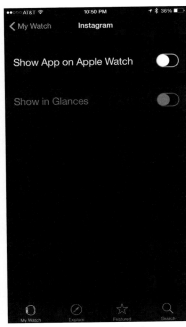

Figure 2.41 The list of currently installed iPhone apps that have an Apple Watch app.

Figure 2.42 Install one by toggling on "Show App on Apple Watch." This app happens to also have a glance.

Toggle this option off to remove the app from your watch.

Arranging your Home screen

The Home screen will get cluttered with apps pretty quickly. And as they install there isn't any order, which drives Bob a little nuts (he likes things in their place at all times). Bob is in luck, because you can arrange apps on your watch in two ways: directly on the watch and through the Apple Watch app.

To arrange your apps on the watch itself:

1. Press the Digital Crown until you're on the Home screen.

2. Force touch the display and the app icons will grow a little and start to wiggle (wiggling is difficult to capture in a screen shot, but you'll know it when you see it).

3. Tap and hold on an app you'd like to move. It'll move above your fingertip (**Figure 2.43**). Without lifting your finger off the display, drag the icon where you'd like to place it. The other icons will move out of the way automatically. Once it is in position, lift your finger and the icon will be moved.

Figure 2.43 You can arrange the app order on Apple Watch by dragging and dropping.

4. Repeat until you're happy with the layout. Press the Digital Crown to settle all the icons down.

To do the same thing on your iPhone:

1. Launch the Apple Watch app.

2. Tap App Layout.

3. Press on the app icon you want to move, and drag it into its new location (**Figure 2.44**).

4. Take your finger off the display and the app will be moved. The change will be reflected on your watch's app screen instantly.

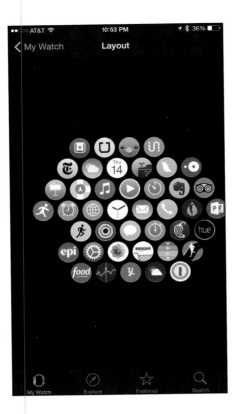

Figure 2.44 The Apple Watch app lets you sort your apps on a bigger screen.

Removing apps

There are two ways to remove apps from your Apple Watch. As mentioned earlier, you can toggle the "Show App on Apple Watch" setting on each individual app through the Apple Watch app.

You can also remove apps on the Apple Watch itself:

1. Push the Digital Crown until you're on the Home screen.

2. Force touch the display.

3. Each app you can remove (all the apps that aren't installed on your Apple Watch by default) will have an X displayed on them (**Figure 2.45**).

4. Tap the X and you'll be asked if you're sure you want to delete the app.

Figure 2.45 Tap the X to uninstall an app.

5. Tap Delete App and the app will be removed from your watch. The app is still installed on your iPhone, so you can always reinstall it (or delete it from your iPhone as well).

Telling Time

Now that Bob has his Apple Watch oriented correctly, he wants to make it reflect his personality. You can do this by selecting a certain band, but there is a limit to the number of bands you can buy. However, it is easy to swap out the watch face on the Apple Watch.

To change the watch face:

1. Make sure the time is displayed on your watch and force touch the watch face.

2. This takes you to the watch face selector (**Figure 2.46**). Swipe left or right to see each of the available watch faces.

Figure 2.46 The watch face picker allows you to select from the available faces.

3. When you see one that you like, tap on it, and Apple Watch immediately sets it as your new watch face.

Apple Watch doesn't support third-party faces just yet, so you only have the stock faces to choose from (see **Table 2.1**). However, you'll notice that some of the watch faces show additional pieces of information. As I mentioned earlier, these little areas that show the date, or your next appointment, are known as *complications*. Apple has borrowed the idea from traditional watchmakers. Complications, in the traditional watch world, are little extras that require engineering tricks to accomplish. One of the most popular complications on a wind-up watch is displaying the phases of the moon.

The Apple Watch complications take that same idea but update it for the smartwatch age. The 10 complications that can be added to some faces (see the "Customizing Your Watch Face" section in a moment) are as follows:

- **Activity:** A quick display of your Activity progress for the day (see the section "Activity" in Chapter 3).

- **Alarm:** Set alarms by tapping on the little alarm icon this complication adds. The time of your next alarm will also be displayed.

- **Calendar:** Display the next appointment on your calendar.

- **Date:** Display the current day of the week/date.

- **Monogram:** Display a one-to-four-character monogram. Available only on the Color face.

- **Moon Phase:** Display the current phase of the moon.

- **Stocks:** Display real-time quotes for the stocks listed in the Stocks app (see "Stocks" in Chapter 3).

- **Stopwatch:** Start and stop a stopwatch with a tap, right from the face.

- **Sunrise/Sunset:** Display times for sunrise and sunset.

- **Timer:** Create a timer with a tap. When a timer is running, it's shown here.

- **Weather:** Display the current temperature.

- **World Clock:** Display the time in a different location.

Among the watch faces that support complications (see Table 2.1) are two different complication display sizes: small and large. The smaller size is a small square, generally located in one of the four corners of the watch face, that displays a snippet of information. The larger complications are rectangular and display text, like the title of your next calendar appointment. No matter the size of the complication, tapping on it will take you to the full app to see more information. For example, tapping the Activity complication will launch the Activity app. Tap the Digital Crown to return to the watch face.

Currently the only watch faces that are available are the ones that ship with your Apple Watch, and not all of them support customization. Table 2.1 describes the features of each face, and indicates whether it supports customization.

Table 2.1 Apple Watch faces

ASTRONOMY

This watch face gives you a tour of the solar system. By default, it shows your current location on the Earth. Tap the moon or solar system to see the current phase of the moon or where all the planets currently are in the solar system. If you scroll the Digital Crown up or down on any of the face aspects (earth, moon, solar system), you'll travel through time and see the state of those celestial bodies as they were, or as they will be. Tapping on either the moon or the earth allows you to rotate either to check out each heavenly body. This face isn't customizable.

CHRONOGRAPH

A fairly traditional watch face, meant to be used in conjunction with the stopwatch feature. This face features two additional hands: the top measures the total time of your stopwatch, and the lap timer below. You can change the time scale of the lap timer from 60 seconds to 6 seconds. You can also change the color of the face and hands, and you have up to four complications.

COLOR

A simple face that features an accent color of your choosing. You can change the accent color and have up to five complications on this face, including the monogram.

MICKEY

Mickey Mouse points you in the direction of the right time and taps his foot every second. Fun fact: If you have a room full of Apple Watches displaying the Mickey Mouse face, the foot will tap in sync. You can't change anything about Mickey, but why would you want to? You can, however, have up to four complications on this face.

MODULAR

This is the default Apple Watch face, and it packs in a lot of information at a glance. A digital clock with a handful of complications makes this an information-dense face. You can change the color of the text on this face, and add up to five complications.

MOTION

A simple digital clock, the date, and a gently moving image make up this face. Every time you check the time, you'll see a slightly different image. Tap the image to cycle through each background manually. You can choose between three backgrounds for this face: butterfly, flower, or jellyfish. You can also customize how the date is shown: off, just the date, or the day and date.

SIMPLE

Simple, no frills, just a simple watch face. You can choose to have just the three hands, or add in the marks (those are the lines that represent the minutes), chapter marks (which represent the hours), numbers, and other details. This face also allows you to set the color of the second hand and display up to five complications.

SOLAR

As the name suggests, this face displays the position of the sun, based on where you are and the time. If you turn the Digital Crown back or forward, you can see where the sun was at particular times. This face isn't customizable.

UTILITY

Another simple face that you can make more detailed by adding numbers to the pips (which are the marks on the face denoting hours and minutes). You can adjust the detail of this face from just marks to hour and minute numbers. This face also displays up to three complications.

X-LARGE

This is probably the simplest of all the faces: a digital clock that displays only the hour and the minutes. Nothing more, nothing less. You can change the color of the numbers (the hour and minute numbers can be set to different shades of the same color).

Customizing your watch face

Bob wants to change his watch face to the Modular face and customize the complications. To do so:

1. Force touch the watch face to enter into the watch face selector and swipe until you find the Modular face (**Figure 2.47**).

Figure 2.47 The Modular watch face.

2. Taps the Customize button under the face to open the customizer (**Figure 2.48**). The dots at the bottom of the display indicate how many customization screens there are. For the Modular face there are two, which you get to by swiping left and right. The areas impacted by the current customization screen are outlined in green. The first customizer screen allows you to change the color of the watch face. Turn the Digital Crown to see the available color options. The changes are instantly reflected on the watch face.

Figure 2.48 Turn the Digital Crown to change the color of the selected watch face.

Once you've selected the color, swipe left to set the complications (**Figure 2.49**). Turning the Digital Crown will cycle through the complication options for the currently selected complication area, which is outlined in green. The topmost option is always Off, which will display a blank space on that spot of the face. Tap on the other complication areas to set them by turning the Digital Crown.

Figure 2.49 Tap on a complication and turn the Digital Crown to see the available options.

3. Once the customization is complete, press the Digital Crown to return to the watch face and the face will reflect the settings.

Stopwatch

Before she goes to bed, Mary runs a few sprints in the backyard. She used to press a few buttons on her trusty Timex stopwatch to time herself, but now that she has an Apple Watch, why not use it?

To launch the Stopwatch app, press the Digital Crown until you're on the Home screen and then tap the Stopwatch icon (**Figure 2.50**).

Figure 2.50 The Stopwatch app icon.

By default, the analog stopwatch face is shown (**Figure 2.51**). Tap the green button to start the clock. The digital readout tells you the total time elapsed, with the large orange handle sweeping across the second dial. The smaller dial tracks minutes.

Figure 2.51 The analog stopwatch face. Tap the green button to start the timer.

With the clock running, the Start button turns red and becomes the Stop button (tap it to stop the clock; tap again to reset). The white button on the right is the lap button. Tap it to log your first lap. When you do, a second blue hand appears that tracks your lap time (**Figure 2.52**). Tap the lap button each time you complete a lap.

Force touching the display brings up the stopwatch mode picker (**Figure 2.53**).

The digital face gets rid of the clock face and shows you the total time elapsed with lap times listed below (**Figure 2.54**). Tap the Start button the start the clock (it turns into a Stop button when the clock is running). Tap Lap whenever you complete a lap. A green dot indicates the current lap.

Figure 2.54 The digital stopwatch clearly displays lap times.

Graph keeps the Start/Stop and Lap buttons and a digital readout of the time elapsed, but it adds a graph of the lap times (**Figure 2.55**). A yellow dotted line appears after you've recorded two laps. This line represents the average time for all the laps so far.

Figure 2.55 The graph face makes it easy to see the differences in the lap times.

The Hybrid view combines all three views into one information-dense stopwatch face (**Figure 2.56**).

Figure 2.56 Hybrid brings all the best aspects of each face into one.

Alarms

Anyone's first day with the Apple Watch is slightly exhausting since it's so exciting. It is bedtime at the Peterson house, and now that everyone has a fancy new watch, why not use them to wake up on time? Keep in mind that there is only one alarm sound on your Apple Watch, though it also gives haptic feedback, which is quite noticeable on your wrist. If the watch is charging, it'll shimmy a little on the table as the alarm goes off.

As you might expect, you can set multiple alarms on your Apple Watch, and there are a few ways to get to the Alarm settings:

- If you have the Alarm complication on your watch face, just tap it to enter a new alarm.
- Tap the Alarm icon on the Home screen (**Figure 2.57**).

Figure 2.57 The Alarm app icon.

All of your current alarms are displayed, along with a toggle to turn them on and off (**Figure 2.58**). Tap on a green toggle to turn off an existing alarm; tap on a gray toggle to turn one on.

Figure 2.58 The list of alarms. The 24-hour clock option is enabled in this screen shot.

Force touch to see the New Alarm button (**Figure 2.59**). Tap it to create a brand new alarm (**Figure 2.60**).

Tap the Change Time button to set the time for your alarm (**Figure 2.61**). Tap on the hour and turn the Digital Crown to set it. Tap on the minutes and turn the Digital Crown to set them as well. Tap Set.

Figure 2.59 Force touch to get to the New Alarm button. Tap to add a new alarm.

Figure 2.60 The alarm options.

If this is an alarm you'll use more than once a week, set it to repeat. Tap the Repeat button and tap each day you want the alarm to repeat on (**Figure 2.62**). You can select any combination of days. Tap Repeat at the top to return to your alarm settings.

Figure 2.61 Setting the time of an alarm is easy: turn the Digital Crown.

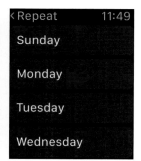

Figure 2.62 Tap the days on which you want the alarm to repeat.

You can label an alarm by tapping the Label button and speaking the name you'd like to give the alarm. Tap Done and the label will new appear on the button.

Finally, you can toggle off the Snooze option, in case you don't want to be able to take advantage of the snooze feature.

When you're done, press the Digital Crown to leave the Alarm app.

▶ **TIP** Tap on any existing alarm to edit it. Scroll to the bottom of the alarm settings and tap Delete to get rid of any unwanted alarms.

Clock settings

There are a few clock-related settings that I'd like to tell you about.

If you like to set the time ahead, you can do so on your Apple Watch. All of your notifications and reminders will pop up at the correct time, but the displayed time will be x minutes fast, where x is anything between 0 and 59 minutes. To do this:

1. Press the Digital Crown until you're on the Home screen and then tap the Settings icon.

2. Tap Time and you'll see the Set Clock Face Display Time Ahead screen (**Figure 2.63**). Tap the gray bar.

Figure 2.63 You can set the clock ahead, so you'll never be late again.

3. Turn the Digital Crown to set the time ahead and then tap Set to apply it (or tap Cancel to discard your change).

The Apple Watch iPhone app also has a couple of clock-related settings:

1. Launch the Apple Watch iPhone app on the paired iPhone and scroll until you see the Clock icon. Tap it.

2. Here you can toggle a variety of settings:

   - **24-Hour Time:** When this setting is on, your watch will display the digital time in 24-hour format (the analog watch faces aren't impacted by this setting).

   - **Push Alerts from iPhone:** Toggle this on to be able to snooze/dismiss alarms set on your iPhone.

   - **Notifications Indicator:** When you have a new notification, a red dot appears at the top of the watch face by default. Toggle this setting off and the red dot will not appear.

- **Monogram:** Tap on this to enter a one-to-four-character monogram, which is displayed on the Color face's monogram complication. Emoji cannot be used in the monogram, sadly.

- **City Abbreviations:** Tap here to change the abbreviations for the cities listed in the world clock (**Figure 2.64**).

Figure 2.64 The list of cities available in the World Clock complication.

Locking

You can manually lock your Apple Watch so that it'll be locked even when worn on your wrist. Billie sometimes does this to her watch so her brother doesn't mess with it while she is taking a nap.

To lock your watch:

1. Hold in the Side button.

2. Slide your finger across the Lock Device button (**Figure 2.65**).

A blue lock icon appears indicating that the watch will require the passcode before you can access any funtions other than telling the time.

Figure 2.65 You can lock your Apple Watch at any time.

Figure 2.65 You can lock your Apple Watch at any time.

Charging

It was a busy day of setting up Apple Watches in the Peterson house, and so the family is going to call it a night before they delve into the Apple Watch tomorrow. The Apple Watch is an electronic device, and as such it needs to be charged every night. The watch does last a good while between charges. According to Apple you should get 18 hours of normal usage before you need to charge your Apple Watch.

▶ **NOTE** All of these numbers come from Apple's website: https://www.apple.com/watch/battery.html

There is a power-saving mode called Power Reserve that allows the watch to work for up to 72 hours on a single charge, but to accomplish this, every feature other than displaying the time must be turned off. This turns your smartwatch into a normal watch.

Expect about a full day's usage out of your Apple Watch. When it is running low on power, you'll be notified to charge it (**Figure 2.66**).

Figure 2.66 If you see this alert, it's time to charge your watch.

Charging the Apple Watch is simple:

1. Plug the provided USB adapter into an outlet.

2. Plug the magnetic charging cable into the adapter and place the round magnetic charger end wherever you'd like your watch to lay as it is charging (Bob has his on his nightstand; Mary keeps hers on her dresser).

3. Take your Apple Watch off and bring the back of the watch close to the concave side of the magnetic charger. It'll latch onto the back and start charging, as indicated by a small lightning bolt icon on the watch face and a chime (unless the watch is muted) (**Figure 2.67**).

Figure 2.67 The lightning bolt means your watch is charging.

▶   **TIP** If you have the Apple Watch charger box, the instructions are pretty much the same. Be sure to keep the charging case open as the Apple Watch charges, though, as it needs to be well ventilated.

When you charge your Apple Watch, it automatically locks itself (which means it'll ask for a password if you try to use it). A locked Apple Watch will not display notifications, so they will be displayed on your iPhone.

You can, of course, use your Apple Watch when it is charging. You'll need to enter the passcode fairly often, since the Apple Watch automatically locks when it isn't on your wrist.

It'll take about 1.5 hours to charge your Apple Watch to 80 percent full, and requires 2.5 hours to get a full charge. This is if you use the included power adapter. You can also charge your Apple Watch by plugging the magnetic charging cable into a powered USB port (either on a computer or a powered USB hub), but using this method charging your Apple Watch will take longer.

CHAPTER 3

Morning

Lots of things happen in the morning, and your Apple Watch can help with many of them. Right from waking up until you start pondering lunch, your Apple Watch acts as a constant companion and helper…though, as the Petersons will find out, the Apple Watch quickly fades into the background, alerting you to things only when you need to know them.

This chapter covers some of Apple Watch's built-in functionality such as setting alarms, tracking activity, and viewing and accepting calendar invitations. I'll discuss some third-party apps (along with links to them in the App Store) that add to or complement functionality on Apple Watch. This chapter also shows you how to manage notifications and glances both on the watch and via the Apple Watch app on the paired iPhone.

Dismissing Alarms/Snoozing

Bob set an alarm for 6 a.m. before he want to bed, and now it's about to go off. When any alarm sounds two things happen: the watch makes an alert sound and it uses haptics to tap you. When the watch is on your wrist, it'll feel like the watch is tapping you, but when it is charging the haptics cause it to vibrate.

When the alarm goes off, the time and two buttons are displayed: Snooze and Dismiss (**Figure 3.1**). By default, Snooze is enabled on all alarms. Tap it and the alarm is silenced to 10 minutes, letting you catch a little more sleep.

When an alarm goes off you can dismiss or snooze.

Figure 3.1 Tapping Dismiss turns the alarm off.

> ▶ **TIP** You can use your Apple Watch to dismiss and snooze alarms set on your iPhone as well. Make sure that you have "Push Alerts from iPhone" enabled in the Apple Watch > Clock section. With that enabled, when an alarm goes off on your iPhone it also buzzes on your Apple Watch. You can dismiss and snooze it from either your phone or your watch.

Louder alerts and stronger taps

Bob is slightly hard of hearing, so he wants to make sure that he'll hear and feel the alerts that his Apple Watch is making. There isn't a volume knob on the watch, but you can use the Settings app to adjust how loud the alerts are and how strong the haptic feedback is:

1. On the Home screen tap the Settings icon and then tap Sounds & Haptics.

2. Tap the left speaker icon to lower the watch's volume and tap the right speaker to increase it (**Figure 3.2**). As you tap, the watch will play a preview sound (and haptic tap) so you can judge when it is loud (and strong) enough.

Figure 3.2 Adjust how loud and how firmly your watch taps you.

Scroll down to the Ringer and Alert Haptics to lessen or strengthen the haptic taps (tap left to lower and right to increase). Once again, a sound and tap previews each setting.

Enable Prominent Haptic to make sure you don't miss out on any common notifications (**Figure 3.3**). When this is enabled, you'll get an additional haptic tap to announce the regular haptic tap of several common alerts.

Figure 3.3 Prominent Haptic double-taps you to make sure you never miss a notification.

► **TIP** Both of these settings can be adjusted via the Apple Watch iPhone app in the Sounds & Haptics section.

To Shower or Not to Shower

Bob is wide awake now, so he straps his Apple Watch on and heads to the shower. He pauses for a moment, trying to decide if it's wise to shower with Apple Watch still on his wrist.

Apple Watch isn't waterproof; it is, however, water resistant. This means that sweat, washing your hands, and splashing water on your watch won't hurt it (it might cause some trouble with the leather bands, since they're leather and all). Apple does not recommend submerging the Apple Watch for any length of time, so no swimming with the watch on.

Apple Watch does have a water resistance rating of IPX7, which means that it is okay to immerse it in water of up to 1 meter in depth for 30 minutes. Given this rating, showering with the Apple Watch should be fine. Bob isn't much of a risk taker, though, so he takes his off (as do I) before he showers. His notifications can wait until his shower is done.

Review Calendar

As Bob is showering, Mary checks out her appointments on her watch.

There are two ways to quickly see your next appointment:

- If you have the Calendar complication on your watch face, just look at the watch face.

- Swipe up from the bottom of the display to enter the glances. Swipe until the Calendar glance is displayed (**Figure 3.4**).

Figure 3.4 An event on the Calendar glance.

Tapping either of these indicators takes you to the full Calendar app, which mirrors the calendar settings on your iPhone. To change the notifications just for the watch, go into the Apple Watch app on your iPhone and select Custom under Calendar (**Figure 3.5**). You can then turn off calendar alerts altogether on the watch, or choose to toggle off Upcoming Events, Invitations, Invitee Responses, and Shared Calendar Alerts notifications.

Figure 3.5 Customizing your calendar alerts allow you to only see what you want to see.

Tap "Mirror my iPhone" to revert back to getting the same notifications on your watch as you do on your iPhone (though only when your iPhone isn't locked).

You can also get to the Calendar app with these steps:

1. Press the Digital Crown until you're in the App screen.

2. Tap the Calendar icon, which always displays the current day and date (**Figure 3.6**).

Figure 3.6 The Calendar app icon.

Once you're in the Calendar app, a list of your calendar events are displayed (**Figure 3.7**). Swipe up and down to scroll, or turn the Digital Crown. The next upcoming event is displayed at the top of the list with the name of the event and the duration. You'll notice a colored bar next to it. This indicates which calendar this event is on, should you have multiple calendars.

Figure 3.7 The Calendar in list view.

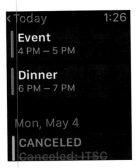

Tap on an event to see more details, including the name of the event and the location. If this is an event that you've invited people to, you'll see yourself listed as the organizer and the list of responses: Accepted, Declined, No Reply (**Figure 3.8**). Keep in mind that all of the attendees will be listed in No Reply until they accept or decline. If no one declines, then the Declined section doesn't appear, as in Figure 3.8. There is also a Notes field, which will have the text of the meeting invitation if any was included.

Figure 3.8 An event's details.

If this is an event on your calendar to which you've been invited you'll see something a little different in the event details (**Figure 3.9**). The organizer will be listed—that's the person who invited you to the event—along with your response to the invitation. Below your current response are three buttons: Accept, Maybe, and Decline. Your current response is highlighted. Tap any of the other two to change your response. If you tap Decline, the event will be removed from your calendar.

Figure 3.9 The options available on any meeting requests you receive.

There is one more way to view your events in the Calendar app: Day view. Force touch when you're on the event list and two buttons will appear: Day and Today (**Figure 3.10**). Tapping Today will always bring you back to the current date on your calendar (more on why you might need this in a second). Tapping Day presents you with a list of all the hours in the day with your appointments displayed on it (**Figure 3.11**). The List view, which is the default view, condenses the day down and shows you only events whereas the Day view shows you the entire day so you can get a sense at a glance of how much free time you have between meetings.

Figure 3.10 The other calendar view, Day, and Today, which always takes you to the current day when tapped.

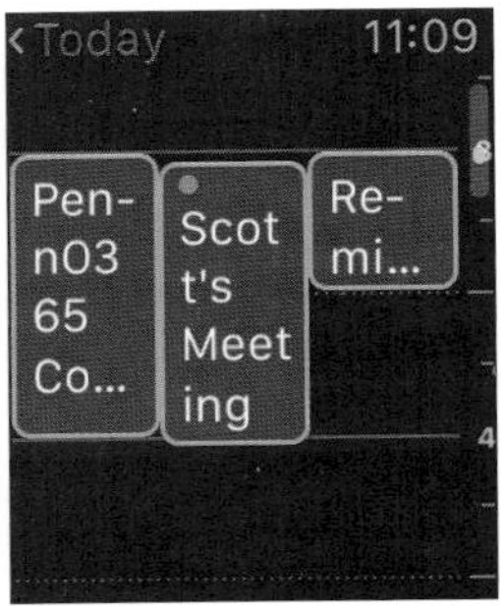

Figure 3.11 The Day view.

To return to the List view, force touch and tap the List button.

At the top of every event screen, the day of the event appears (sometimes this'll say Today, or the actual date if the event is in the future). Tapping on this brings you to the month view (**Figure 3.12**), which lets you easily hop between days in the calendar.

Figure 3.12 The month view. Tap a day to see the events.

If you get too far afield and want to return to Today's appointments, force touch and tap Today.

Calendar complication

The Calendar complication can be added to a number of watch faces. It has two sizes that display different amounts of information:

- `1:00AM📅`: The small complication displays the time of your next upcoming meeting. Tap it to go to that event on your calendar.

- `1:00AM EVENT`: The larger complication displays the event's title as well as the time on your watch face. Tapping it also opens your calendar to that event so you can see even more information.

▶ **TIP** If you're double-booked for a particular time slot, an exclamation point will be displayed in the complication.

Running late

If you're running late for a meeting, your Apple Watch makes it easy to send the organizer a quick note:

1. Tap the event on the Apple Watch calendar app.

2. Scroll until you see the organizer. Tap on the organizer (as long as it's someone other than you) (**Figure 3.13**).

Figure 3.13 Contact details.

3. If the organizer is in your contacts, you can tap the phone icon to call them, or you can tap the bubble icon to send them a text message.

▶ **TIP** If the organizer's phone number isn't in your contacts, your watch will send an email with the selected message from step 4. The email will come from an address that will send any replies as a text message to your phone/watch.

4. Tapping the bubble icon brings up a list of pregenerated texting options (**Figure 3.14**). Scroll through and tap one to send it off. You can also send emoji or dictate messages; those are covered in the next chapter's "Text Messaging" section.

Figure 3.14 Pregenerated messages.

You can also email the sender of the meeting request:

1. Open the meeting on your Apple Watch.

2. Force touch the meeting/event and an Email Sender button appears (**Figure 3.15**).

Figure 3.15 Force touch any event you've been invited to in order to email the sender.

3. Tap the button and you'll see the options in Figure 3.14.

▶ **TIP** If a meeting has an address in the Location field, you can easily get directions. Open the meeting on your watch and force touch it. A Directions button appears. Tap it to get directions from your current location to the meeting location (as long as it's an address).

Accepting meeting requests

Mary finishes looking at her calendar and gets out of bed. She feels a tap on her wrist and sees that she's just been invited to a meeting (**Figure 3.16**). Keep in mind that *you* decide if you want to see calendar notifications on your watch. If you've disabled the notifications you won't be notified, clearly, but the event will go on your calendar where you can tap on it (as described earlier) and respond.

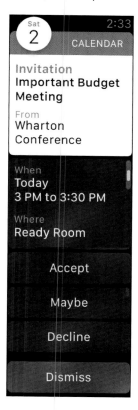

Figure 3.16 A meeting invitation.

The notification allows Mary to Accept, Decline, or list herself as a Maybe. Tapping any of those options sends off a notification to the meeting organizer (assuming your Apple Watch is connected to your iPhone). Tapping Accept adds the event to your calendar, whereas tapping Decline sends the notification but doesn't add the event to your calendar since you won't be going. Tapping Maybe adds the event to your calendar as well, but it's displayed with a striped background (**Figure 3.17**). This indicates that you've tentatively accepted. If you tap the event and scroll down you're able to accept or decline.

Figure 3.17 Tentative meetings appear with a striped background.

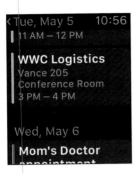

Adding events on your watch

Apple Watch doesn't have a keyboard for text input, and none of the apps offer one. This is because typing on a screen that size wouldn't be pleasant. This may lead you to believe that creating an event on Apple Watch is impossible. Not so. You can create events, even events with additional attendees, right from your wrist.

To create an event on your watch:

1. Press and hold the Digital Crown until Siri appears.

2. Say "Schedule Dinner at 8 p.m. on Friday" and Siri will think about it for a moment.

3. If there's a conflict Siri will ask you if you want to schedule it anyway (**Figure 3.18**). Tap Yes and the event will be added to your calendar. If there's no conflict, Siri will show you the appointment she thinks you want to add (**Figure 3.19**). Tap Confirm to add it.

▶   **TIP** You can also say, "Add dinner" or "Create a new event called Dinner...." Siri is pretty clever.

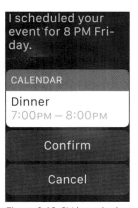

Figure 3.18 A calendar conflict alert from Siri.

Figure 3.19 Siri has scheduled your event, but you need to tap Confirm to add it to your calendar.

If you want to invite one of your contacts to a new event from your watch, do the following:

1. Launch Siri by pressing and holding the Digital Crown.

2. Say "Schedule Dinner with Joe at 8 p.m. on Friday." If you have more than one Joe in your contacts, Siri will ask you which one you meant (**Figure 3.20**). Tap the correct Joe.

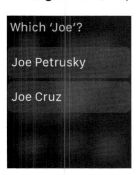

Figure 3.20 Select which person you meant by tapping the name.

The event will be created and an invitation sent.

If you try to schedule something with someone who isn't in your contacts, Siri just adds the name to the event title, so "Dinner with Joe" would be the title of the event.

All of the events created by Siri are added to your default calendar and invitations are sent from the email account associated with that account. If you only have one calendar on your iPhone this doesn't matter, but if you're syncing multiple calendars (perhaps a Google Calendar and an Exchange calendar for work), you'll want to make sure the events are added to the correct calendar.

To check your default calendar, tap the Settings app on your iPhone and then tap Mail > Contacts > Calendars. Scroll to the Calendar section and tap the Default Calendar (**Figure 3.21**).

Figure 3.21 The Default Calendar is where all your created events end up.

Meeting reminders

Mary has her iPhone set up to notify her of meeting reminders (which are usually set for 15 minutes before the meeting is scheduled to begin, but can be set to something else by a crafty meeting organizer). Since those notifications are set up, they appear on her watch when her phone is locked (**Figure 3.22**). Tap the Snooze button to delay the reminder for 5 minutes and tap Dismiss to get rid of it entirely. Tap the notification to see the location of the meeting and the time it is scheduled.

Figure 3.22 A meeting reminder.

Stocks

Billie is getting into the stock market and wants to stay up on the stocks she's been trading on a fantasy stock exchange. Apple Watch includes a Stocks glance and a full-blown Stocks app to keep you up to date with your investments. The stocks will update when the watch is connected to an iPhone. Stock information will still be displayed otherwise, but it won't be current.

To glance at stock information:

1. Go to the clock face and swipe up.

2. Swipe left or right until you see the Stocks glance (**Figure 3.23**). By default the glance displays the current price of the default iPhone stock. Tap it to open the Stocks app.

Figure 3.23 The
Stocks glance.

You can open the Stocks app by

- Pressing the Digital Crown until you get to the Apps screen, and then tapping its icon (**Figure 3.24**).

Figure 3.24 The
Stocks app icon.

- Pressing and holding the Digital Crown until Siri starts and then saying "Open Stocks"

The Stocks app lists all the stocks that are tracked on your iPhone stock app (more on that in a second). For at-a-glance information, if a stock is up it's displayed in green, and if it's down it'll be in red. You can scroll through the list and tap on a stock to get more information.

▶ **NOTE** All the stock information is provided by Yahoo!.

Customizing the Stocks app and glance

Billie wants the glance to show her Google's current stock price instead of Apple's. To do this:

1. On the paired iPhone, launch the Apple Watch app.

2. Scroll until you get to the Stocks section of the apps list and tap on it (**Figure 3.25**).

3. Here you can turn off the glance entirely, which we don't want to do. You can also see that Default Stock is set to Mirror iPhone. Tap that and the list of stocks in the iPhone Stocks app are listed (**Figure 3.26**).

The stock currently displayed in the glance has a check next to it. If you don't see the stock you want to add here (in this case GOOG is listed), it needs to be added to the iPhone Stock app. Once it's added, it'll show up here.

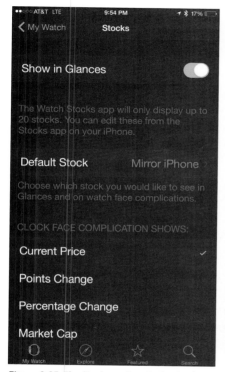

Figure 3.25 The Stocks settings in the Apple Watch app.

Figure 3.26 You can change the default stock for the watch separately from your iPhone.

4. Tap GOOG (or whatever stock you want displayed in the glance). The check moves to indicate that stock will now be displayed in the glance.

You can also set what's displayed in the stock complication here. It'll display whatever is set as the default (for Billie it is now Google). The complication can display Current Price (the default), Points Change, Percentage Change, or Market Cap. Tap whichever you want in the Clock Face Complication Shows section (see Figure 3.25). The check mark indicates the current setting.

Weather

Since everyone needs to get dressed before heading out, all the Petersons want to know what the weather for the day is going to be. Luckily, Apple Watch comes with a built-in Weather app that's pretty good.

The Weather glance shows the current temperature and conditions along with a high and low temperature for the watch's current location (**Figure 3.27**). Tap the glance to launch the full Weather app for more information.

Figure 3.27 The Weather glance shows you the weather in your current location.

The Weather app uses a clever clock face interface to show what the conditions are going to be over the next 12 hours (**Figure 3.28**). Tap it to show the temperature over the same period (**Figure 3.29**) and once more to show the chance of rain (**Figure 3.30**).

Figure 3.28 The Weather app uses a clock metaphor to show conditions over the day.

Figure 3.29 The high temperature throughout the day.

Figure 3.30 Chance of precipitation.

► **TIP** Force touch on the Weather app to bring up three buttons that let you hop between these three weather views.

Scrolling reveals the 10-day forecast.

At the bottom of the display you'll see some dots. These dots indicate that there are more cities listed in the Weather app. The default screen is the weather in your current location (as determined by your iPhone's GPS). Swipe left to cycle through the rest of the locations listed, which mirror the locations in the Weather app on the paired iPhone.

To change the default city (which is listed first in the app, shows up in the glance, and is displayed in the weather complication on watch faces):

1. Launch the Apple Watch app on your pair iPhone and tap Weather.

2. Tap Default City (**Figure 3.31**).

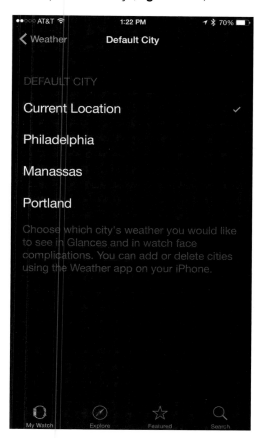

Figure 3.31 Set the default city for the Watch Weather app in the Apple Watch app.

3. All of the cities listed in the iPhone Weather app are displayed, with the current default city checked. Tap the city you want to be the default and you're done. If you'd like to make a city that isn't on the list the default, you'll first need to add it to the iPhone's Weather app and then make it the default here.

▶   **TIP** To add more cities, add them in the Weather app on the iPhone and they will show up on your watch.

Alternate weather apps

There are two other weather apps that you should consider adding to your watch: Yahoo Weather (free; http://apple.co/1eoNjZL) and Dark Sky ($3.99; http://apple.co/1jbFV23).

The Yahoo Weather glance shows you the current temperature and conditions but it also features a "feels like" temperature, the chance of rain, and the wind speed for your current location (**Figure 3.32**).

Figure 3.32 Yahoo!'s weather glance displays the temperature, a feels-like temp, precipitation percentage, and wind speed.

The full Yahoo Weather app (which you can get to by tapping on the glance or launching it via the Apps screen) gives you the same information, but as you scroll it displays sunrise and sunset information and a weather timeline for the next 24 hours (including what the temperature will be in the morning) (**Figure 3.33**).

Dark Sky is a little different in that it doesn't have the fancy graphics you'll find in the stock Weather app or the Yahoo Weather app, nor does it show you weather information for a list of cities. Dark Sky only tells you the weather for your current location, based on GPS.

Figure 3.33 The Yahoo Weather app continues the minimalistic look.

The glance displays the current temperature, a forecast for the next hour, and either how many hours of daylight are left or how many hours before the sun rises (**Figure 3.34**).

Figure 3.34 Dark Sky is all about the weather in your current location.

The full app gives you the same information in the first screen (with an animation) (**Figure 3.35**). If you swipe left, you'll go through the current day's weather data and the 5-day forecast for your current location. Scroll to get an hourly breakdown of conditions, including the likelihood of precipitation per hour.

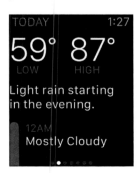

Figure 3.35 The Dark Sky app tells you when it's going to start raining.

The focus on weather in your current location means that Dark Sky probably isn't going to be the only weather app on your Apple Watch, but this hyper focus on local conditions enables Dark Sky killer features: notifications when it is about to rain. Since Dark Sky only concerns itself with weather in your immediate area, it can be used to send notifications when it's beginning to rain (you set these notifications on the iPhone app). This is great when you're about to walk out the door and then you get a tap on your wrist reminding you to grab an umbrella.

Dealing with Notifications

Apple Watch is great at displaying notifications, but the display can get a little crowded with notifications after a bit of time. You can clear away notifications one by one, or en masse right from the watch itself. And you can manage which apps send you notifications from your iPhone.

▶ **TIP** Sometimes you'll find that tapping on a notification doesn't do anything. This means that the notification comes from an app installed on your iPhone but not on your watch. The app may not be available for your watch.

Dismiss

Swipe down from the top of the display to see all the notifications on your Apple Watch (**Figure 3.36**). As was discussed previously, you can scroll through these notifications to read them. Tap to see more information about the notification, if it has a corresponding Apple Watch app installed. The notifications are displayed in reverse chronological order, with the most recent notification displayed at the bottom of the list. Scroll up to see previous notifications.

Figure 3.36 Notifications can start to pile up.

To dismiss a notification:

1. Swipe down from the top of the watch face to show the list of notifications.

2. Swipe left on the notification you want to dismiss and a Clear button appears (**Figure 3.37**).

Figure 3.37 Slide left and tap the Clear button to dismiss notifications one by one.

3. Tap the Clear button and the notification is no longer displayed.

If you have a bunch of notifications and you want to clear them all, it would be super annoying if you had to swipe them away individually. Luckily, you can easily clear all notifications:

1. With the notifications displayed, force touch the display.

2. Tap the Clear All button that appears (**Figure 3.38**). All of the notifications will be cleared.

Figure 3.38 Force touch to bring up the Clear All button.

▶ **TIP** When you're in a notification, you can dismiss it by swiping down.

Managing notifications

By default Apple Watch mirrors all the notification settings of your iPhone. If you have an app set to display notifications (banner or pop-ups) on your iPhone, those notifications will appear on your watch when the iPhone is locked.

To check out your notification settings for the apps on your iPhone:

1. Tap the Settings icon on the paired iPhone.

2. Tap Notifications and you'll see a list of all the apps on your iPhone and their current notifications settings (**Figure 3.39**). The list has two sections: Include and Do Not Include. The apps on the Do Not Include section will not cause notifications on your watch by default.

Figure 3.39 Notification settings are determined on the iPhone.

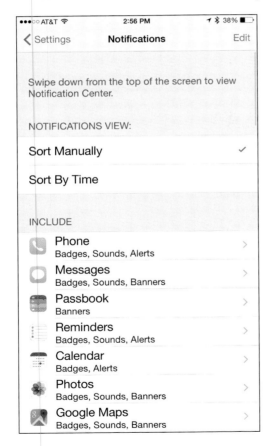

If you want a third-party app (that is, not an app that's built into Apple Watch) to show notifications on the watch, the notifications must be enabled here.

Conversely, you might want to have some apps show notifications only on your iPhone, but Apple Watch mirrors notifications by default. You can change this setting in the Apple Watch app on your iPhone:

1. Launch the Apple Watch app on your iPhone and tap Notifications.

2. Scroll down until you see the Mirror iPhone Alerts From section (**Figure 3.40**). Listed here are all the apps on your iPhone that can send notifications. When toggled on (that is, the button is to the right and showing green), those notifications will show up on your Apple Watch. Tap to toggle it off (or tap on an off notification to toggle it on). This allows you to have iPhone apps that only notify you on your iPhone.

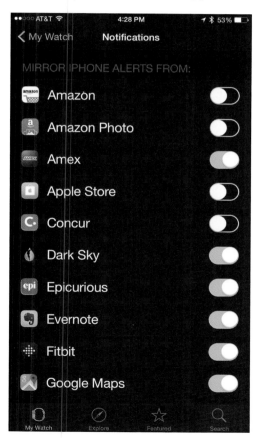

Figure 3.40 Toggle on and off notifications in the Apple Watch app.

The built-in apps, however, do not have such limitations (it is good to be Apple). All of the Apple Watch apps that complement built-in iPhone apps mirror notifications by default, but you can customize them so that you, for example, get notifications of new email on your watch but not on your iPhone. Here's how:

1. Launch the Apple Watch app.

2. Scroll down until you get to the built-in apps list (which starts with Activity). Tap on the app whose notifications you want to change (Mail in this case).

3. Mirror is selected by default, and below that are the details as to what this means on your watch (**Figure 3.41**). Here you can see Mail won't show any notification of alerts on my watch because it doesn't alert on my phone. Tap Custom to change this.

4. Each custom section will be slightly different but all will include Show Alerts (**Figure 3.42**). Toggle this on (or off) to specify whether you want this app's notifications to show up on your watch.

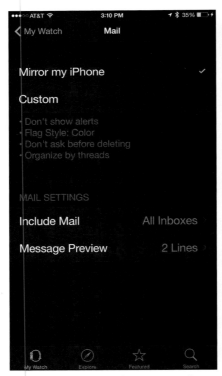

Figure 3.41 The Mail notifications mirror the iPhone settings by default.

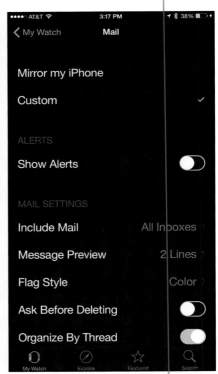

Figure 3.42 Customizing the Mail notifications makes sure only the email you care about taps you on the wrist.

Apple Watch has been designed from the ground up to give you little bits of glanceable information. Notifications do this by appearing on the display as you raise your wrist and showing you the icon of the app sending the notification and then the text of the alert.

You might not want the text of messages or emails to display automatically for everyone who can see your watch to read. You can set notifications to show only the icon of the app sending them and then require a tap to see the text of the alert. To do this:

1. Launch the Apple Watch app on your paired iPhone and tap Notifications.

2. Enable Notification Privacy by tapping the button next to it (**Figure 3.43**).

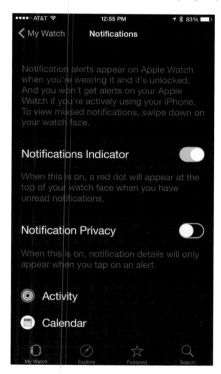

Figure 3.43 Turn Notification Privacy on in case you don't want everyone to see the text of your notifications.

Now when you get a notification, the icon of the notifying app will be displayed and you'll need to tap on it to read the text of the notification.

Reviewing Your Inbox

Once Mary is done checking out her calendar, she needs to delve into her email to do a little inbox triage. She could pick up her iPhone and delete, forward, and reply to email, but then she always gets sidetracked by typing a long reply and never gets finished with cleaning up her inbox.

Apple Watch is great for looking through your email, deleting things you don't need, and marking things for follow-up. What makes it so great at this? The fact that you can do all of those things is impressive, but the fact that you can't do one thing makes it easy to focus on inbox management: reply and compose email.

The Apple Watch Mail app does not support composing or sending email; it's just for reading, marking, and deleting messages.

► **TIP** Even Siri will refuse to compose an email for you on Apple Watch.

Email notifications on the watch match those on your iPhone, by default, and the Watch app displays a combined inbox with email from each of your email accounts in one list.

To get to your email on Apple Watch:

1. Press the Digital Crown until you're on the Home screen. Tap the Mail icon (**Figure 3.44**).

Figure 3.44 The Mail app icon.

2. Email from all your email accounts on your iPhone will be displayed in a list (**Figure 3.45**). Scroll with your finger or by turning the Digital Crown.

Figure 3.45 Email from all your inboxes on your wrist.

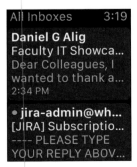

The first line displays the sender; under that is the subject line, followed by a two-line preview of the content. A blue dot next to the sender indicates that message is currently unread.

While in the list view, if you swipe right on a message two buttons appear: More and Trash (this may be an Archive button depending on what kind of email account you're checking) (**Figure 3.46**). Tapping Trash deletes the message. Tapping More calls up two more options: Flag and Mark As Unread (or Mark As Read if the selected message is unread).

Figure 3.46 Swipe left on a message to reveal the Trash and More buttons.

Tapping Flag makes an orange dot appear next to read messages or outlines the blue unread indicator with orange for read messages (**Figure 3.47**). This flag will propagate across linked email clients, so these messages will be flagged in Mail on your iPhone and on your Mac.

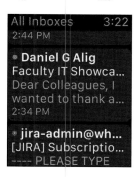

Figure 3.47 The orange dot indicates that a message has been flagged.

For example, Mary flags any messages that require a response on her watch. When she gets to her Mac, she has a special filter set up in Mail to show only flagged messages so she can reply to them quickly.

Tap a message to read it (**Figure 3.48**). Scroll through the message using your finger or the Digital Crown. Force touch to trash/archive, mark as unread, or flag the message you're viewing (**Figure 3.49**).

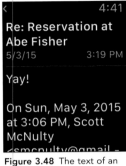

Figure 3.48 The text of an email message.

Figure 3.49 Force touch on a message to flag it, mark it unread, or delete it.

Scrolling all the way to the top of the message shows you the sender information. Tap on it to see who sent the email and who they sent it to (**Figure 3.50**). If the sender or the receiver is in your contacts, tapping their name will bring up their contact. Tapping a sender/receiver who isn't in your contacts will take you to a similar screen, but the only option available is to send a (text) message to their email address.

Figure 3.50 Mail message details.

If you opt to do this, you'll be able to compose the message just like you do with a normal text message, except that it won't be delivered to another phone number but rather sent to that email address. Check your carrier's documentation about what format the text will appear as and what the from email address will be (usually it is something like your cell number@carrier's special email text domain.com).

Tap Info > Details to get back to the message. Tap the < to get back to the email list.

▶ **NOTE** Mail on the Apple Watch only displays text emails. If you try to view an HTML email on the watch you'll get a message about how the message can't be rendered on the watch. Scroll down for the text version (**Figure 3.51**).

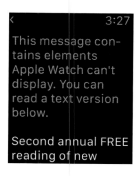

Figure 3.51 HTML email messages can't be displayed on the watch.

Customizing Mail

Right out of the box, notifications for Mail on your Apple Watch mirror those on your phone, and the mailbox displayed is the combined inbox with a two-line preview. All of these things can be customized to make your Mail experience on the watch more enjoyable. Mary doesn't want to see all of her email on her watch; she wants to see just those messages that are from important people in her life.

This can be done by leveraging the VIP mailbox feature and changing some settings in the Apple Watch app:

1. First off, you need to tell your iPhone who the important people are whose email actually matters to you. To accomplish this, you need to set up the VIP mailbox. Launch Mail on your iPhone and go to the Mailbox list (**Figure 3.52**).

2. Tap VIP. This will list all the VIPs currently represented in this mailbox, along with an Add VIP button at the bottom of the list (**Figure 3.53**). If you're adding your first VIP, only the Add VIP button will appear.

3. Tap the Add VIP button and your Contacts list appears. Scroll or search for the contact you want to make a VIP and tap that name.

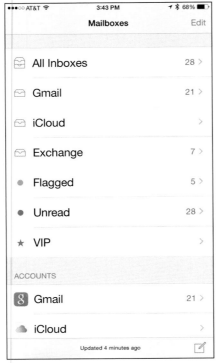

Figure 3.52 The iPhone Mailbox list.

Figure 3.53 Setting up a VIP mailbox.

4. That person is added to the VIP list. Tap Add VIP to add more people to the list.

    When you return to the Mailbox list, you'll notice that there's an I in a circle next to the VIP mailbox. When you tap on the VIP mailbox, you'll see all the messages from the contacts you've designated as VIPs. To add new VIPs to a VIP mailbox, just tap that new I icon and then tap Add VIP.

5. Mary has her VIP mailbox set up on her iPhone, so now it's time to change the mailbox that the Apple Watch displays. Launch the Apple Watch app on the iPhone and tap Mail.

6. Under Mail Settings, tap Include Mail.

7. All of your mailboxes are listed here (**Figure 3.54**). You can select only one mailbox to be displayed on your Apple Watch, but you aren't limited to the boxes listed at the top of the screen. If you scroll down to the Accounts section and tap on an account, you can set the watch to display email from a folder from any of your email accounts.

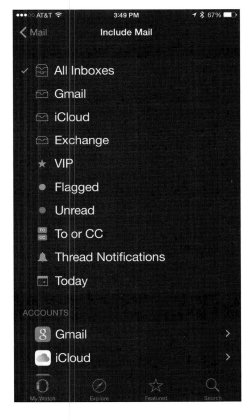

Figure 3.54 Select a mailbox to display on your watch.

Since Mary wants to display her VIP mailbox, she taps that and that's what will show up on her Apple Watch.

8. Tap > Mail to return to the Mail Settings and tap Message Preview. You have three options: None (no preview) , 1 Line, or 2 Lines. No Preview will make the email list the most compact, but you'll have to tap each message to see what is in it.

Now if you launch Mail on your Apple Watch, only email from VIPs will be displayed (noted in blue at the top of the list), and only those emails will result in notifications (**Figure 3.55**).

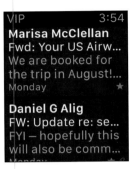

Figure 3.55 The blue title shows you which mailbox is being displayed (VIP in this case).

Custom Notifications

Mary has particular needs for her mail usage on her Apple Watch. However, if you want to have all your new email messages show up on your watch but you don't want to be notified about each on your watch, take these steps:

1. Launch the Apple Watch app and tap Mail.

2. Tap Custom until the Notifications to see all the options you have (**Figure 3.56**).

- Show Alerts is a global on/off for Mail alerts. Toggle it off and no Mail alerts will appear on your watch.

- Each email account has a separate on/off toggle for alerts.

- VIP alerts you only when someone on that list emails you.

You can have any combination of those options by toggling them on and off.

Figure 3.56 Custom
mail notifications
make sure you see
what you want to see
on your watch.

Managing Glances

Billie has installed a bunch of apps on her Apple Watch and enjoys the
quick hits of information she gets when swiping up on the watch face. But
there are a few glances that were installed by apps, or installed by default,
which she just doesn't find useful. Plus, it would be really great if she could
change the order around a bit so that the glances she uses most are right
next to each other to limit the amount of swiping she has to do.

Both removing and reordering glances are supported, but you have to do them via the Apple Watch app on the paired iPhone:

1. Launch the Apple Watch app on the paired iPhone.

2. Tap Glances and you'll see a list with two parts: currently active glances and Do Not Include (which are inactive glances available to your watch), as shown in **Figure 3.57**.

Figure 3.57 Glances can be removed by swiping and tapping Remove.

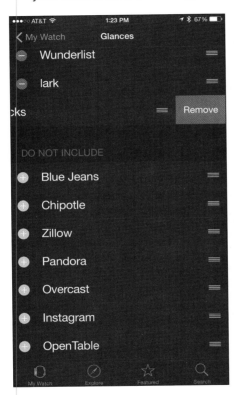

3. Tap the red minus icon next to an active glance. This will reveal a Remove button. Tap it and the Glance will be moved to the Do Not Include section. Tap the green plus icon next to any glance in the Do Not Include section to activate it. This is a one-touch operation, but if you tap by mistake, just tap the red minus and then tap Remove to move the glance back.

The list of active glances is shown in the order that the glances are arranged on your watch. Next to each glance is a button that looks like three parallel horizontal lines (**Figure 3.58**). Tap and drag this button to move the selected glance into a new position in the list. You can even move the Settings glance, which defaults to the top, into a new position.

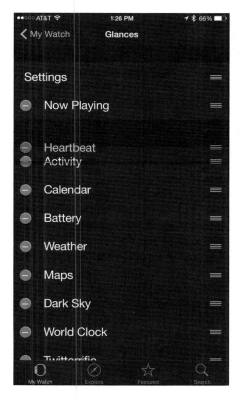

Figure 3.58 Reorder glances on the Apple Watch app by tapping and dragging.

Once you're happy with the glance order, exit the app and your Apple Watch glances will reflect the new order and any activated/inactivated glances will be added/removed.

Any app that includes a glance allows you to turn off that glance in the Apple Watch app. Launch the Apple Watch app, scroll down to the app list, and tap on an app, and you'll see that you can specify whether or not to show the app itself on the watch and determine if the glance should be activated (**Figure 3.59**).

Paying with Passbook

Bob hops into his car after saying goodbye to his family and heads off to work. He almost always stops at Starbucks to get a little pick-me-up, and he's long been a user of the Starbucks iPhone app. The app allows you to pay for your coffee using a barcode that is displayed on the phone, but now that Bob has an Apple Watch he doesn't want to haul out his phone when the future is all about paying for things with his wrist.

▶ **NOTE** Apple Pay, which will be covered in the next section, allows you to pay for things with your watch as well, but it uses your existing credit cards. Apps like the Starbucks app require you to have a balance on a store card to use them.

Luckily for Bob the Starbucks app stores his card information in Passbook on his iPhone. Passbook is designed to store cards, plane tickets, and the like, eliminating the need to have those fobs on your keychain or to tote around physical tickets. You can access everything that is in your paired iPhone's Passbook on your Apple Watch, but the card must be in Passbook first.

To get a Starbucks card into your iPhone's Passbook:

1. Install the Starbucks app on your iPhone (I'm assuming you already have a Starbucks account and a balance on a Starbucks card; if you don't, you'll need both of those things as well).

2. Sign into the app with your username and password and then tap Pay.

3. Here you can add a Starbucks card to your account, but I'll assume you already have one like Bob does (**Figure 3.60**). Your balance is displayed, and you can tap Pay to pay for a coffee right here, but that's not what we want to do. Tap the Manage button.

Figure 3.60 The Starbucks app allows you to check your balance and pay for coffee.

4. Tap the Add To Passbook button and then tap Continue (**Figure 3.61**). You may be asked to add a favorite store, which you can do or skip; it isn't a required part of adding the card to Passbook.

Figure 3.61 Tap Continue to add the Starbucks card to Passbook.

5. A preview of the Passbook card appears along with Cancel and Add buttons. Tap Add and the card slides into your Passbook on your iPhone.

    You can launch Passbook on your iPhone to confirm that it is, indeed listed (**Figure 3.62**).

Figure 3.62 The Starbucks card in Passbook.

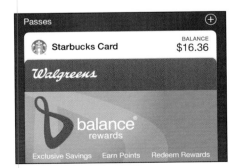

Now that the card has been added to your Passbook it'll be accessible on your Apple Watch. To open Passbook on your Apple Watch, do one of the following:

- Press and hold the Digital Crown to activate Siri and say, "Open Passbook."

- Press the Digital Crown repeatedly until the App screen appears and tap the Passbook icon (**Figure 3.63**).

Figure 3.63 The Passbook app icon.

Your watch's Passbook list may differ slightly from the one on your iPhone, because you have to set up Apple Pay separately for the watch (**Figure 3.64**). At the top are any credit cards available via Apple Pay on your watch with the loyalty/reward/tickets/other cards listed below.

Figure 3.64 Passbook on Apple Watch.

To pay for his coffee at Starbucks, Bob

1. Opens Passbook on his watch.

2. Taps the Starbucks card to see his balance (**Figure 3.65**).

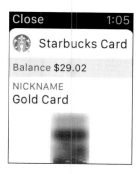

Figure 3.65 The Starbucks card in the watch's Passbook.

3. Taps the Starbucks card again to display a barcode across the entire watch's screen (**Figure 3.66**).

Figure 3.66 Cashiers scan this code to charge your card (the code has been blurred out for this figure).

4. Holds his watch up to the Starbucks scanner, and payment is subtracted from his Starbucks balance—all without ever taking his phone out.

▶ **NOTE** Many stores and chain restaurants support Passbook in their apps. You can use the method just described to pay using Passbook in any of those locations as well. The Starbucks app instructions for adding a card to Passbook are specific to that app, but the steps will be very similar in other apps.

Logging Into Your Work Computer

Bob arrives at work with his coffee and settles down at his desk to do some work. The first thing he has to do is log into his work computer. Bob uses the password manager 1Password (https://agilebits.com/onepassword) to generate and store complex passwords. In fact, Bob's passwords are so complex that he doesn't remember any of them without the help of 1Password (hence the app's name; you need to remember only one password: the password that unlocked 1Password).

Setting up 1Password is beyond the scope of this book, but the iPhone/iPad app does include an Apple Watch app that requires a little setup of its own. But once it's set up, Bob can call up his password on his wrist and type it in without trouble:

1. First you'll need to get 1Password for iPhone (free; http://apple.co/1ewYoCY). Set it up on your iPhone following the on screen directions.

2. Open 1Password and tap the Settings icon (**Figure 3.67**). Tap on Apple Watch.

3. Here you can enable the Apple Watch 1Password app by toggling it on (**Figure 3.68**). You're prompted for a 4-digit PIN that you'll be required to enter when you launch 1Password on your watch. Enter the PIN twice.

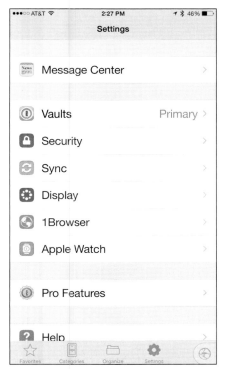

Figure 3.67 1Password iPhone app settings.

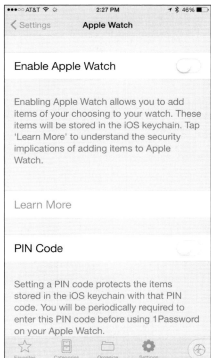

Figure 3.68 You have to enable the 1Password Apple Watch app.

4. Now that the Watch app is enabled, you need to select things from your 1Password vault (that's the term 1Password uses for your collection of usernames, wallet information, and more) that you want displayed on the watch. Tap on a login you want to show up on the watch (in this case

Bob's work login) and tap "Add to Apple Watch" (**Figure 3.69**). That tags the login with Apple Watch.

Figure 3.69 A login in 1Password. Tap Add to Apple Watch to make it available on the watch.

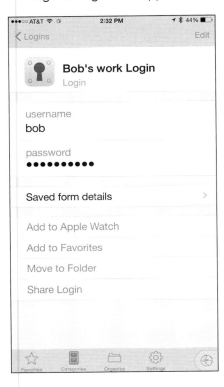

5. Install the 1Password app on your watch by open the Apple Watch app, tapping 1Password, and tapping "Show App on Apple Watch."

6. Tap the 1Password icon on the App screen or use Siri to launch 1Password. You'll be asked to enter the PIN you created (**Figure 3.70**).

Figure 3.70 Enter the 1Password passcode.

7. Enter the PIN and all the logins you added to the Apple Watch are displayed in a list (**Figure 3.71**). Tap on the one you need to enter, and the password and username are displayed right on your wrist for easy typing (**Figure 3.72**). If the display turns off before you finish typing in the password, just tap it to turn it back on.

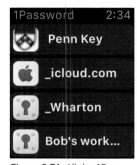

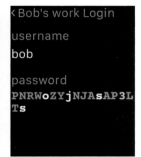

Figure 3.71 All the 1Password entries you choose to make available on the Apple Watch.

Figure 3.72 Your password, on your wrist.

Activity

Mary works from home as an accountant, and she is totally into quantifying everything and anything in her life, including her fitness regimen. Apple Watch also tracks your steps (when you're wearing it) as a component of overall activity levels that are tracked in an app called Activity (**Figure 3.73**).

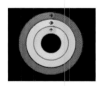

Figure 3.73 The Activity app.

The Activity app uses a bulls-eye metaphor with three rings to track three goals:

- **Movement:** The Move ring is the outermost (red) ring, which tracks how many calories you've burned based on how much you've moved during the day. This is the only goal that you can modify (more on that in a moment).

- **Exercise:** The second (green) ring is the Exercise ring, and this tracks the amount of time you've spent doing any activity (to quote Apple) "that equals or exceeds a brisk walk." The goal for this ring is 30 minutes of exercise, but don't think that you have to go to the gym and sweat it out. A 30-minute walk at a good pace will meet this goal just as well as 30 minutes of flat-out running. You cannot change this goal, though the app will track more than 30 minutes of exercise should you exceed the goal.

- **Standing:** The innermost (blue) ring is the Stand ring, which I think is slightly misnamed. Every hour, if you haven't stood and moved for at least one minute you'll get a reminder telling you to stand. The reminder tells you to stand, so you can earn your "standing" for that hour. If you do this 12 times, over 12 hours in the same day, you meet your standing goal. This goal cannot be altered.

You can launch the Activity app in a few ways:

- If you have the Activity Ring complication on a watch face, tap it to launch the app.

- On the Home screen tap the Activity app icon.

- Swipe up on the watch face to bring up Glances and swipe until you see the Activity glance (**Figure 3.74**). Tap it to open the app.

Figure 3.74 Your activity, at a glance, on the Glances screen.

Both the Activity complication and the glance give you a quick sense of how you're doing with each goal. As you get closer to each of the goals, that ring becomes more and more complete. Once the ring is complete, you've met that particular goal.

The Activity app gives you a lot more detail. The first screen displays the set of rings. Scroll down and you'll find out some detailed information about your activities so far, including the number of calories you've burned, the number of steps you've taken, and your total distance traveled (**Figure 3.75**).

Figure 3.75 The Activity app gives you a lot of detail.

At the bottom of the screen you'll see four dots, letting you know that there are three more screens to see.

Swipe left to see the Move section. The number of calories you've burned since the start of the day (midnight) appears encircled by the red Move ring (**Figure 3.76**), along with your goal. This goal is the only one that you can adjust; read on for directions on how to do that.

Scroll down to see a graph plotting the number of calories burned against the hours in the day (**Figure 3.77**). The spikes should correspond to any strenuous activity you might have engaged in while wearing the watch.

Figure 3.76 The Move ring tracks how many calories you've burned.

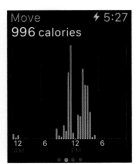

Figure 3.77 The calories charted against the hours of the day.

Another swipe left brings you to the green Exercise ring, which shows your total amount of active minutes and the goal (30 minutes) (**Figure 3.78**). Scroll to see a chart of your active minutes against the hours of the day (**Figure 3.79**).

Figure 3.78 The Exercise ring displays how much exercise you've done.

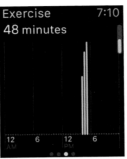

Figure 3.79 More details include when you exercised.

The final screen is dedicated to your total number of "stands," as shown by the Standing ring and the number of stands out of the goal you've already completed (**Figure 3.80**). Scroll to see which hours you've managed to stand for at least a minute (**Figure 3.81**).

Figure 3.80 Standing means moving at least for one minute an hour.

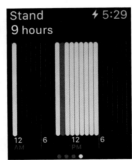

Figure 3.81 Track your standing versus when you stood.

Force touching on any of these screens brings up the Change Move Goal button (**Figure 3.82**). Tap it to change the calorie goal represented by the Move ring (**Figure 3.83**). Tap the plus button to increase the goal, tap the minus button to decrease it, or click Cancel to keep it the same. If you've changed your goal, be sure to tap the Update button.

▶ **NOTE** You cannot change the exercise or stand goals.

Figure 3.82 Force touch to change your move goal (the only goal that can be changed).

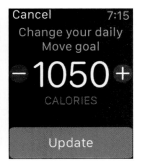

Figure 3.83 Tap -/+ to decrease/increase your goal.

Activity alerts

The Activity app is pretty motivating, but when combined with notifications it can change your behavior. By default your Apple Watch will notify you when you haven't stood for the first 50 minutes of an hour (**Figure 3.84**). You'll also be notified when you meet each of the goals as you go throughout the day (**Figure 3.85**).

Figure 3.84 If you haven't stood up in the first 50 minutes of an hour, you're alerted to stand.

Figure 3.85 Your watch tells you when you've reached a goal.

To modify these notifications:

1. Launch the Apple Watch app on the paired iPhone and tap Activity.

2. Here you're able to do a number of things like turn off the Activity glance and the stand reminders. If you don't want to be notified about goal completions or achievements (more on these in a second), or receive weekly or 4-hour updates, toggle those options off.

Weekly Summary

Once a week the Activity app will display the Weekly Summary (**Figure 3.86**). It displays how often you hit your Move (calorie) goal, along with a chart showing you how you did each day of the week, and the total number of calories, steps, and distance you earned over the week.

Figure 3.86 Every week your Apple Watch displays a summary of your activity.

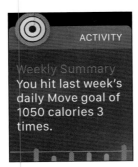

The most interesting thing about the Weekly Summary is that, based on how you did, it suggests a new Move goal for the coming week (**Figure 3.87**). You can increase and decrease this new goal by tapping on the plus and minus buttons and then tapping Set Move Goal. If you want to keep your current goal, tap Dismiss and the goal won't be changed.

Figure 3.87 The summary suggests a new Move goal based on your week's movement.

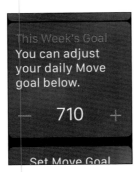

Achievements

Gamification is a theory that says, if I can oversimplify it, it is possible to encourage behaviors by giving out awards or achievements. These achievements do not need to be physical objects in order to be effective, something that the Activity app takes advantage of. You'll be awarded a number of achievements as you use the Activity app. Some are easier to get than others, and they include

- First Workout

- Perfect Week

- Move Goal 200%

Each of these achievements is unlocked when you hit a certain milestone (completing your first workout, hitting all of your goals every day for a week, and moving more than twice your goal during a day). When you get an achievement, you are notified on your watch (**Figure 3.88**). Tap to view the achievement, and then tap Close to dismiss it (**Figure 3.89**). Once you dismiss that notification, though, you aren't able to see your awards on the watch. You need to go to the iPhone Activity app on the paired iPhone and tap Achievements to see all of your awarded achievements (**Figure 3.90**).

Figure 3.88 Achievements are awarded when you reach goals.

Figure 3.89 An achievement (virtual) medal.

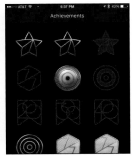

Figure 3.90 All of your achievements are viewable on the Activity iPhone app.

All of the achievements you've earned are displayed in color, whereas the ones you have yet to earn are outlines. Tap on an achievement to see what triggered it and when (**Figure 3.91**). Tapping on an unearned achievement gives you its name and what you need to do in order to unlock it (**Figure 3.92**).

Figure 3.91 You can see the medal and what it was awarded for.

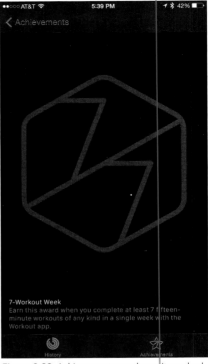

Figure 3.92 Achievements you haven't reached yet are listed.

The iPhone app also allows you to look back at the previous day's activity metrics. When you launch the app, the current day's activity information is shown (**Figure 3.93**). Scroll down to see how you're doing in each of the three rings, as represented by some lovely charts. Swipe left to see the actual metrics for each section (**Figure 3.94**).

The bottom of the activity screen lists any workouts you tracked with your watch (see the next section for more about this).

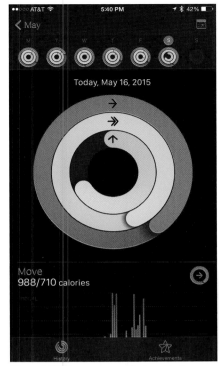

Move 988/710 calories	
Active calories	988
Resting calories	3398
Total calories	4386

Figure 3.93 Your progress displayed in the Activity iPhone app.

Figure 3.94 Your Move metrics.

At the top of the screen are the past week's activity circles. Tap on any of them to review the information from that day. If you want to see a day further in the past, tap the month in the upper-left corner of the screen to go into calendar view (**Figure 3.95**). Each day that has recorded activity is indicated by the good old activity bulls-eye, which also serves as a preview of the activity details you'll find by tapping on one of them.

To return to today's activity from any screen, tap the calendar icon in the upper-right corner.

Figure 3.95 Activity displayed across months.

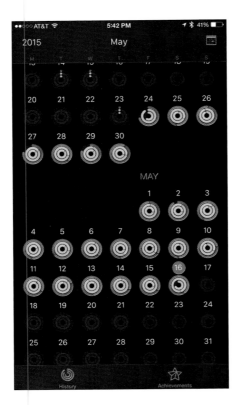

Figure 3.95 Activity displayed across months.

Working Out with the Watch

The Activity app is meant to record your activity as you go throughout your day and encourage you to move a bit more. It doesn't provide any real-time feedback as you're engaged in strenuous exercise, though. That's where the Workout app comes in.

Mary, since she is into tracking things, wants her Apple Watch to help her track her progress on her morning run. All she has to do is go to the Home screen and tap the Workout icon (**Figure 3.96**).

Figure 3.96 The Workout app icon.

All of the workouts that the watch can track are listed, along with the stats from the most recent workout of that type (if any) (**Figure 3.97**). Scroll through the list until you find the workout you're going to do. If you can't find what you're intending to do, select Other, which is at the end of the Workout list.

Figure 3.97 The Workout app can track a variety of workout types.

Once you've selected a workout (Outdoor Run in this case) you need to set a goal:

- Calories
- Distance
- Time
- Open (you just want to exercise)

If you've completed an exercise of this type, your last distance/calorie burn/time are set as the starting goal in an effort to encourage you to set a personal record.

Once you've set a goal of one type (using the plus and minus buttons to enter the number), the Start button becomes active. Tap it and you're given a 3-second countdown, with countdown noises, and then it's off to the exercise races.

The watch now displays the Workout app as you're working out (**Figure 3.98**). The current time is displayed, as well as a progress ring. Along the bottom of the display are several dots indicating that you can swipe to show different pieces of information:

▶ **TIP** If you rather see your progress rendered in numbers and not a ring, go to the Apple Watch app, tap Workout, and toggle Show Goal Metric. It'll update immediately on your watch.

Figure 3.98 Track your progress as you're working out.

Outdoor Run

9:14

00:44.58

Elapsed Time

- **Elapsed Time:** How long you've been exercising.

- **Pace:** If you're running/walking, the watch will tell you what your mile pace is.

- **Distance:** The distance you've traveled (in feet) if you're doing an activity in which distance is relevant.

- **Calories:** The number of calories you've burned. Feel the burn.

- **Heart Rate:** Apple Watch can take your heart rate, and this will display an updated heart rate as you're exercising.

As you're exercising, whenever you bring the wrist up the watch will display the Workout app instead of the watch face if the Workout app is actively tracking some exercise. This is incredibly useful as you're working out because the last thing you want to do is tap around on your watch; swipe to look at the other pieces of information and keep on sweating!

Once you meet your goal, you'll be prompted to end the workout (though you can continue working out if you like). When you end the workout, your Apple Watch will display a summary of your workout, including many details of the exercise (**Figure 3.99**). You can choose to save the workout or discard it. When saved, the workout details are saved in the Activity app; discarded workout information is deleted.

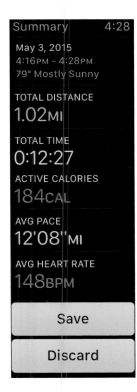

TOTAL DISTANCE
1.02MI

TOTAL TIME
0:12:27

ACTIVE CALORIES
184CAL

AVG PACE
12'08"MI

AVG HEART RATE
148BPM

Save

Discard

Figure 3.99 The workout summary gives you the highlights of your workout.

During the workout, you might want to either pause to catch your breath or just give up on the workout and cancel it altogether. Swipe to the rightmost section to bring up the End and Pause buttons (**Figure 3.100**). Tapping End brings you to the workout summary, where you can decide if you want to toss the data or save it. Force touching during a workout brings up the same buttons, which is far easier to do when you're exercising (and the amount of workout you've already completed is displayed, perhaps to encourage you to stick it out until the end) (**Figure 3.101**).

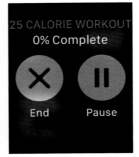

Figure 3.100 Swipe in the Workout app to end or pause a workout.

Figure 3.101 Force touch to bring up the End/Pause buttons at any time.

Heart rate

As you move throughout the day your watch is checking your heart rate (or beats per minute [BMP]) every 10 minutes. It does this by using two sets of LEDs on the back of the watch: one infrared and the other green. Based on the light absorption and science, the watch can determine your heart rate.

To see what your current heart rate is:

1. Swipe up from the clock face to bring up the glances and swipe to the Heartbeat glance.

2. As soon as you open the glance, it forces the watch to check your heart rate (**Figure 3.102**). The time and value of the last check is shown, and the heart animates as the check is being done.

Figure 3.102 The Heartbeat glance measures and displays your current heart rate.

Once the check is done, your current BPM is displayed (**Figure 3.103**).

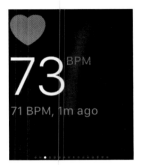

Figure 3.103 The author's heart rate.

There are a couple of things you should be aware of with the heart rate sensor on Apple Watch:

- It works best when the watch is snug on your wrist. If the watch is too loose, the sensors can't determine your heart rate.

- If you have tattoos covering your skin where your Apple Watch is resting, the heart rate sensor may not work. Since it depends on measuring light bouncing off your blood, the dark inks in tattoos can confuse the sensors.

To view all of the heart rate data that your watch is collecting, you'll need to look on the Health app on the paired iPhone (**Figure 3.104**). Your watch transmits that data to the iPhone for storage. To check it out:

Figure 3.104 The Health iPhone app icon.

1. Tap the Health app icon to launch it.

2. Tap Heath Data on the bottom of the screen and then tap Vitals (**Figure 3.105**).

3. Tap Heart Rate (your watch can only measure your heart rate at the moment, though you can pair other sensors with it to measure more things) to see your heart rate data (**Figure 3.106**).

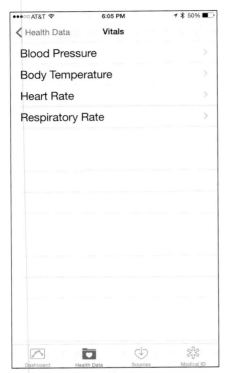

Figure 3.105 The Health app aggregates your health data in one place.

Figure 3.106 The Vitals section of the Health app.

Tap Day, Week, Month, or Year at the top to change the scale of the chart displaying your heart rate. The chart plots the highest and lowest value of your heart rate against the time scale you select.

Tap Show All Data to see a list of every heart rate measurement your iPhone has on record (**Figure 3.107**). All of the measurements from the watch will have a blue watch icon next to them, along with the BPM value and the date and time they were taken.

Tap on one to see even more detail about the date and time of capture and when this information was added to your iPhone (**Figure 3.108**).

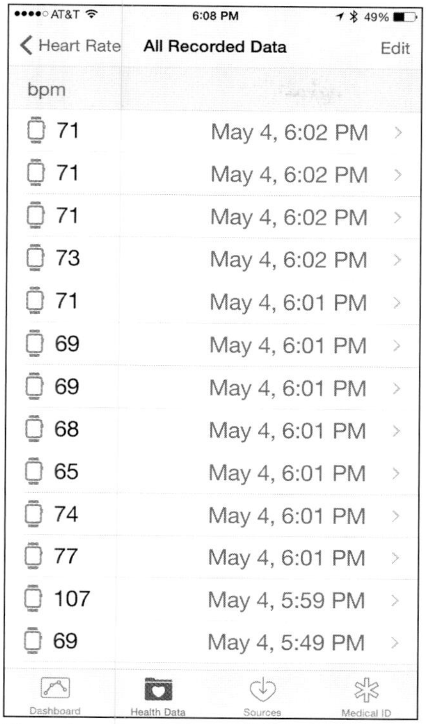

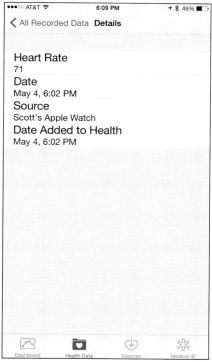

Figure 3.107 Apple Watch stores all of the heart rate measurements in the Health app.

Figure 3.108 Tap on an entry to see when it was captured.

Tap the Edit button at the top of the screen to delete any of the data points you'd like (**Figure 3.109**). The Clear All button at the top left will delete all of the heart rate information from the Health app.

▶ **TIP** Apple Watch does support Bluetooth heart rate monitors if that's your thing.

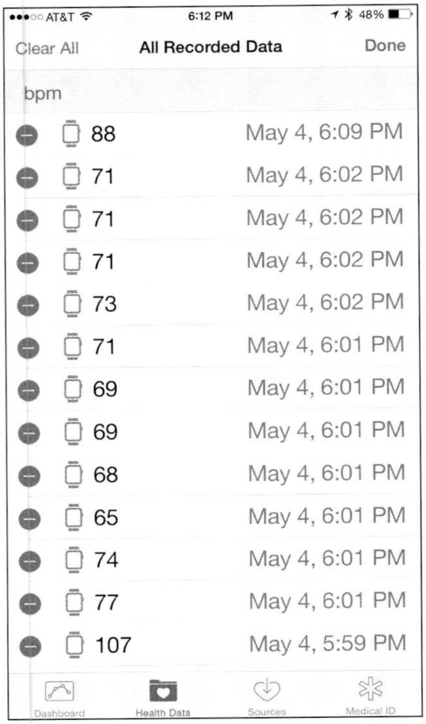

Figure 3.109 Tap Edit to delete individual entries.

The heart rate sensor starts to check a little more often when you're walking or exercising, in order to keep the active calorie metric as precise as possible. The downside to this is that it can negatively impact the watch's battery life. If you're okay with potentially inaccurate calorie measurement in exchange for longer battery life, you can disable the heart rate sensor during these activities by following these steps:

1. Launch the Apple Watch app.

2. Scroll until you see the Workout entry and tap it.

3. Toggle on Power Saving Mode (**Figure 3.110**).

Now the heart rate sensor will automatically turn off when your watch senses that you're walking or running.

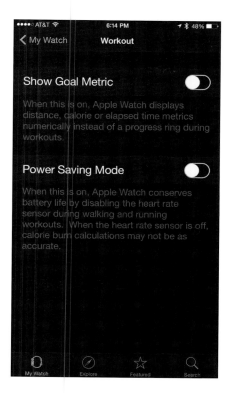

Figure 3.110 Power Saving Mode disables the heart rate sensor while you're working out to conserve battery life.

Calibrate

Apple Watch uses a bunch of data, including GPS and other sensor information, to accurately measure your active minutes and caloric burn. However, you might notice that it doesn't record as many active minutes, or steps, as you think you've been making. You can calibrate your Apple Watch to make sure it is more accurately recording your stride, which in turn, makes all the other metrics more accurate.

To calibrate your Apple Watch's activity tracking:

1. On a nice clear day grab your Apple Watch and the paired iPhone and head outside to a nice, flat place: a local high school track or park will do nicely. This will ensure that your Apple Watch can use your iPhone's GPS to accurately track your speed and determine your stride.

2. Double-check that Location Services is enabled on your iPhone (Settings > Privacy > Location Services). When enabled, this option allows your iPhone to tell apps (like the Workout app on your watch) where you are. Also make sure that the Motion Calibration & Distance setting is on (Settings > Privacy > Location Services > System Services). Without this option enabled, your iPhone can't figure out your stride.

3. To accurately measure your stride you need to either hold your iPhone in your hand or strap it to your waist or arm using a iPhone band case.

4. Tap the Workout app on your watch and then tap Outdoor Walk. Set it for a 30-minute walk, and then tap Start.

5. Walk at a constant rate for 30 minutes. The calibration process happens automatically as you walk.

6. Repeat this as often as you like to ensure that the Workout app knows your stride.

▶ **NOTE** This is totally optional; Apple Watch is pretty good at figuring out your stride by itself. The calibration just helps the process along.

Workout app alternatives

There are lots of apps that will track exercise for you, though Apple Watch is best suited to track aerobic exercise in which your location changes (like running and bicycling). When you use the Workout app to track an outdoor run/walk/bike ride, it leverages GPS (assuming you bring your iPhone along with you) to accurately measure the distance you've covered. What it doesn't do, and what many people like to do, is map your workout.

RunKeeper (free; http://apple.co/WKXaBD) has an Apple Watch app that allows you to track and map your runs, so you can save favorite routes and see how much ground you've covered.

Install the RunKeeper app on your iPhone, and then install the Apple Watch app. RunKeeper does require an account to use, so set that up on your iPhone and then you're ready to track your first outdoor run/walk/bike ride:

1. Launch the RunKeeper app on your Watch (**Figure 3.111**). It doesn't allow you to set goals; there's just one button that you tap to start running.

Figure 3.111 The RunKeeper wants you to go running.

2. When you tap the Start Run button, you will hear your iPhone will say, out loud or over your headphone, "Activity Started." That's your signal to start running/walking/biking.

3. The RunKeeper app will continue to run in the background of your watch, but if you raise your arm to check it out as you run you'll see the watch face. Go to the Home screen and tap the RunKeeper app to see your run's duration, how far you've gone, and your minutes per mile (**Figure 3.112**).

Figure 3.112 RunKeeper as you run.

As you run you'll hear audio cues that tell you, at intervals, how far you've run. You can set what audio cues you'd like to here in the iPhone settings (more about that in a moment).

4. Tap Pause and then tap Stop to end your run.

5. Tap Save and the data is saved to the RunKeeper service via your iPhone.

Change the Wrist Activation Behavior

By default whenever you lower your Apple Watch and then raise it again, you'll see the watch face. This means that if you're looking at an app's screen and then lower your arm, the next time you raise your watch you'll see the time. If you press the Digital Crown twice, you'll be taken back to the last app you were using.

Generally, this is what you want to happen, but when you're using an app to track a run this behavior becomes inconvenient. It's easy enough to change, both on the watch and via the Apple Watch app.

On the watch:

1. Go to the Home screen and tap the Settings icon.

2. Scroll down to General and tap it. Then tap Activate On Wrist Raise.

3. Scroll to the Resume To section and tap Last Used App (**Figure 3.113**).

On the Apple Watch app:

1. Launch the Apple Watch app and tap General.

2. Scroll down to Activate On Wrist Raise and tap it.

3. Tap Resume Previous Activity (**Figure 3.114**).

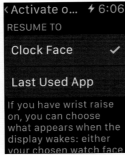

Figure 3.113 When you raise your wrist, the watch displays the clock face. You can change it to display the last used app.

Figure 3.114 On Wrist Raise can also be set via the Apple Watch iPhone app.

Now when you raise your wrist the last active app will be displayed. To change back to the watch face, repeat the previous steps but tap Show Watch Face on the iPhone or Clock Face on the Watch.

To view your workout, you'll need to launch the RunKeeper iPhone app and follow these steps:

1. Tap Me at the bottom left of the display (**Figure 3.115**).

Figure 3.115 The RunKeeper iPhone app stores all your runs.

2. This screen is a sort of Dashboard view of your RunKeeper profile (**Figure 3.116**). Tap on the Activities section to see more details about the runs you've kept (**Figure 3.117**).

Figure 3.116 A RunKeeper profile.

Figure 3.117 A list of runs in the app.

3. Tap on a run to see the details, including the map of the route you took (**Figure 3.118**). Tap on the map to see it full screen. RunKeeper will also show you splits (to see if you're improving mile over mile) and charts (which display your elevation, number of steps, and more all drawn against the precise time of your run).

To change the audio cues that RunKeeper provides as you run:

1. Tap the Settings icon in the bottom-right corner of the RunKeeper app Home screen.

2. Scroll down until you see Audio Cues. Tap it to turn on and off a variety of audio cues designed to keep you motivated (**Figure 3.119**).

3. Tap Back and then tap Audio Timing to set the cues to be spoken at time-based or mileage-based intervals.

The settings are saved automatically.

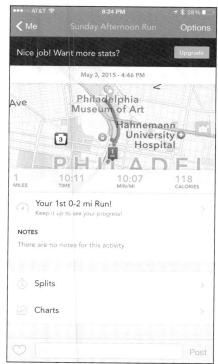

Figure 3.118 RunKeeper displays some details and a map of your run.

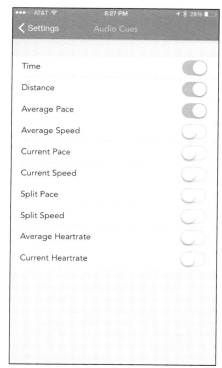

Figure 3.119 Set the audio cues in the iPhone app.

▶ **NOTE** The RunKeeper app is free, but you can upgrade to their Pro level to get a number of additional features, including the ability to compare workouts, training plans, and live broadcasting of your route so people can keep up with your workouts in real time.

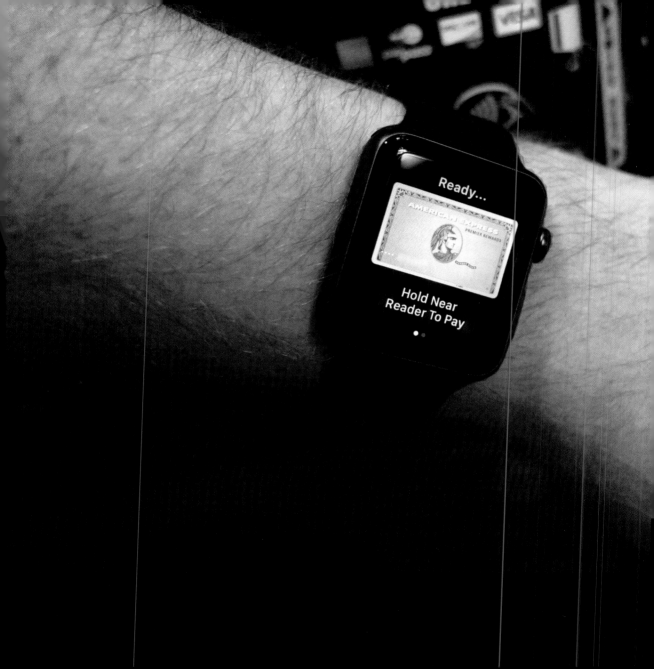

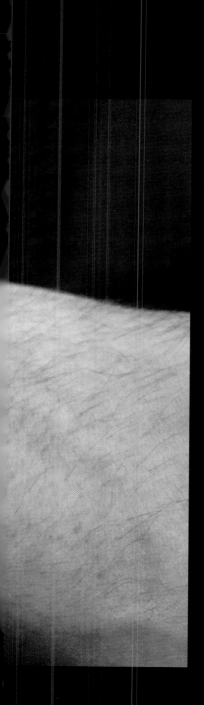

CHAPTER 4

Afternoon

The afternoon is upon us, and all the Petersons are hard at work either in the office, the home office, or at school. This section will delve into the communication abilities of Apple Watch, including calling, texting, and using Digital Touch to reach your contacts. This section also covers how to set up and use Apple Pay on your watch, and more.

Making Phone Calls

While at the office Bob has to make lots of phone calls, and he generally does so from his iPhone. However, since Bob has a new toy in his Apple Watch, he wants to use it as often as possible. Apple Watch can make phone calls, and you can even talk to people by holding the watch up to your mouth much like Dick Tracy. There are a few things to keep in mind about Apple Watch telephony:

- It requires that the paired iPhone be in range.

- Apple Watch only has a speaker phone, unless you've paired a Bluetooth headset to it (more on that later).

- All phone calls initiated from your Apple Watch actually come from your iPhone, so that's the number people will see on their caller ID.

To call someone in your contacts from your Apple Watch:

1. Press the Digital Crown until you're in the Home screen.

2. Tap the Phone app icon (**Figure 4.1**).

Figure 4.1 The Phone app icon.

3. The Phone interface appears (**Figure 4.2**). Your favorites, recent phone calls, and contacts are all listed here.

Figure 4.2 You can access favorites, recent calls, contacts, and voicemail right from your watch.

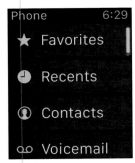

Favorites mirrors your favorites on your iPhone (**Figure 4.3**). Tap here and then tap the favorite that you want to call.

Figure 4.3 Favorites mirror those on your iPhone.

Recents lists all the recent phone calls you've received or made (**Figure 4.4**). If the call was from/to a contact, that person's name and the label of the number involved with the call is displayed. Outgoing calls are denoted by a small telephone icon, whereas incoming calls have no icon. Any calls in red represent missed calls. Tap any of these to call that person/number.

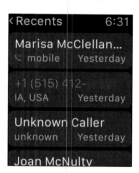

Figure 4.4 Recent calls. Any in red are missed calls.

Contacts allows you to scroll through your entire contact list using your finger or the Digital Crown (**Figure 4.5**). Tap on a contact to see their picture (if one is assigned to them) and two contact buttons: call and text. Tap the call button and Apple Watch will make the call (**Figure 4.6**). For contacts with multiple phone numbers you'll first have to tap the phone number you want to call (**Figure 4.7**).

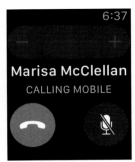

Figure 4.5 Your phone's contacts are accessible on your Apple Watch.

Figure 4.6 The phone call screen allows you to mute and cancel a call.

Figure 4.7 If a contact has more than one number associated with them, you must tap the number you want to call.

4. When your friend picks up, tell them all about how you're talking to them from your wrist.

While you're on the phone call, the duration of the call is displayed, along with a volume bar, a call end button, and the mute button (**Figure 4.8**). Tapping the mute button mutes your microphone, and tapping the call end button ends the call.

Figure 4.8 When you're on a call, tap the red button to hang up. Turn the Digital Crown to adjust the volume.

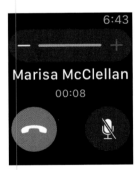

Since this call is actually being placed via your iPhone, your friend's phone will display your normal phone number (your Apple Watch doesn't have a number of its own). If you turn on your iPhone's display, you'll notice a green banner at the top of the screen that says "Touch to return to call" (**Figure 4.9**). If you tap on this banner while you're on a phone call via your Apple Watch, the phone call will transfer to your phone, seamlessly. This is called Handoff, and it's a feature that, well, hands off various activities from one device to another.

Figure 4.9 Calls originate on your iPhone, so you can easily switch devices by tapping the green banner.

Calling someone using Siri

You can also call people just by telling your Apple Watch to do so. Siri, Apple's voice-powered assistant, is able to make phone calls on your behalf. This is great when you're driving or you just don't want to have to follow as many steps to make a call. To use Siri to call folks:

1. Press the Digital Crown until Siri is activated.

2. Say "Call *someone in your contacts*" where *someone in your contacts* is a person in your contacts.

3. If there is only one match to the name and there is only one phone number associated with that contact, Siri will place the call immediately. If there are multiple matches (name or phone number), all of the matches will be displayed (**Figure 4.10**). Tap the one you meant. If there are no matches, Siri will display an error (**Figure 4.11**).

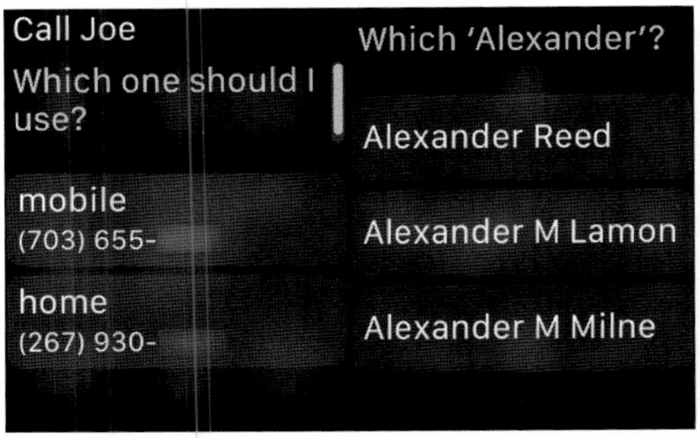

Figure 4.10 Siri can make calls, but if there are contacts who share names, or have multiple numbers, she needs a little help.

Figure 4.11 If Siri can't find the person in your contacts, you'll get this error message.

► **TIP** To call someone who isn't in your contacts, simply activate Siri and say "Call…" and speak the numbers of the phone number (including the area code). Siri will call the number.

Answering calls

It stands to reason that if you can make calls from your watch, you can answer them as well. When your iPhone receives a phone call it will ring, just as it normally does (respecting whatever ringtone/vibration settings you have made), but your Apple Watch will also ring and tap you on the wrist.

If someone in your contacts is calling, their name and phone number displays on the screen along with two buttons: decline (red) and accept (green) (**Figure 4.12**).

Figure 4.12 Incoming calls display the name of the contact who is calling.

> ▶ **NOTE** If the person calling you isn't in your contacts, just the phone number will be displayed.

Tapping the green button accepts the call and takes you to the phone call interface, where you can mute, change the volume, and hang up.

Tapping the decline (red) button sends the caller straight to voicemail.

Voicemail

Bob always declines any call from an unknown number, so he gets a lot of voicemail. He can check his voicemail without having to fish his phone out of his pocket by following these steps:

1. Press the Digital Crown until the Home screen is displayed and tap the Phone icon.

2. Tap the Voicemail button.

3. Your watch displays your list of voicemails, with the most recent first (**Figure 4.13**). The name or number of the person call is displayed in white, with the duration of the message and the date underneath in gray. Tap on a voicemail entry.

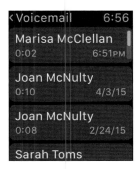

Figure 4.13 The Voicemail list includes the name of the contact and the length and date of the message.

4. Here you see some information about the voicemail you've tapped, along with two buttons: call and delete (**Figure 4.14**). Tap the call button to call the number who left the voicemail and tap the delete button to delete the voicemail completely.

Figure 4.14 Tap the play button to listen to the voicemail. The green button calls the contact back; the red button deletes the voicemail.

Right in the center of the screen is the play button. Tap it and you're taken to the voicemail playback screen (**Figure 4.15**). The voicemail starts to play, and you can adjust the volume by tapping the plus and minus buttons at the top or by turning the Digital Crown.

The two buttons at the bottom of the screen skip back 5 seconds (left) and forward 5 seconds (right).

Force touch or tap the name of the contact/phone number to return to the previous voicemail screen, where you can delete the voicemail.

Figure 4.15 When you're playing back a voicemail, use the Digital Crown to adjust the volume.

▶ **TIP** When you tap the Delete button on a voicemail, it is deleted immediately without a confirmation. However, it can still be retrieved in the voicemail app on your iPhone. Tap on the Deleted Messages folder on your iPhone to see a list of deleted voicemails.

When you receive a voicemail, a notification appears on your watch (**Figure 4.16**). Tap it and there's a playback control right in the notification (**Figure 4.17**). Tap the play button to listen to it and scroll down, and you'll find Call Back and Message buttons. Tapping the Message button allows you to send a text message in reply.

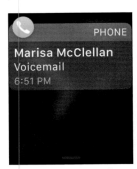

Figure 4.16 A voicemail notification.

Figure 4.17 Tap on the notification and you can play the voicemail right there.

Text Messaging

Billie and Aaron hardly ever use their iPhones to place voice calls; they are all about the texting. They text their friends, they text each other, and they text their parents. Apple Watch is a great way to be notified about text messages (**Figure 4.18**). Just tap the Reply button to reply to a text message, right from the notification.

Figure 4.18 The text message notification includes a Reply button.

When you tap the Reply button, a list of suggested messages appears (**Figure 4.19**). Scroll to see the whole list. If one of the messages listed is appropriate, tap it and it is immediately sent. This list of suggestions is pretty clever in that it will try to offer contextual options. If there is a question in the message you've received, some common answers to questions appear at the top of the list (**Figure 4.20**). If the message includes a question with two options like "Do you want to get sushi or hamburgers for dinner?" sushi and hamburgers will both be on the list (**Figure 4.21**).

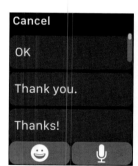

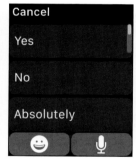

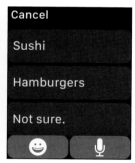

Figure 4.19 The list of stock text messages.

Figure 4.20 The Messages app is smart and offers contextual options based on message contents.

Figure 4.21 If you are texted with an either-or question, both options are on the reply list.

This is all designed so you don't have to type in a text message, since you can't (darn that lack of a keyboard!). However, you can dictate a text message should any of the prepopulated options don't fit the bill. To dictate a text message reply:

1. Tap Reply in the text notification to get to the text composition screen (see Figure 4.18). Tap the microphone icon.

2. You're now on the familiar Siri screen. Start talking and Siri will transcribe what you're saying and preview it on the display (**Figure 4.22**). If Siri mistypes something, or you want to check the text, sadly the only option is to hit the Cancel button and start over. Keep in mind that you have to speak your punctuation as well—if you still use it, that is.

3. When you're happy with your message, tap Send. What happens next depends on who you're texting. If the person you're texting is an iPhone/Apple Watch user, that means more than likely they are using iMessage. iMessage is a lot like text messaging, but Apple has added a layer of additional functionality to it. Another very important thing to know about iMessages: they don't count against any text messaging plans that you might have.

   You iMessage people using their phone numbers, or email addresses, and Apple Watch can sense if this phone number is an iMessage number. If it is, you get two options to send your message (**Figure 4.23**). You can choose to send it as an audio file, which the receiver will then play and hear your lovely voice. Or you can send your text message as a plain old, well, text message.

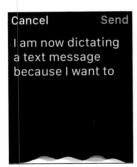

Figure 4.22 Dictate custom messages using Siri.

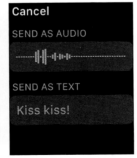

Figure 4.23 If you're sending an iMessage, you can send your message as text or as an audio file.

If the number you're texting isn't an iMessage number, the text will be sent as plain text automatically, saving you a tap.

▶ **TIP** You can tell your watch to always send to iMessage using audio or text by launching the Apple Watch app on your iPhone and tapping Messages and then Audio Messages. Tap either Always Dictation or Always Audio and you won't be prompted to choose anymore.

Changing the Default Replies

The list of default replies that you can send with a tap can be customized. For example, if you often text the phrase "Roger, roger" you can replace one of the default messages with that.

This can only be done on the paired iPhone:

1. Launch the Apple Watch app on the paired iPhone and tap Messages.

2. In the Messages screen, tap Default Replies (**Figure 4.24**).

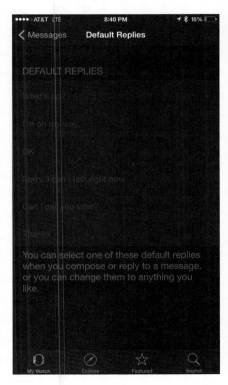

Figure 4.24 The Default Replies can be customized via the Apple Watch app.

3. The list of six default replies is shown. Tap on one to replace it (**Figure** 4.25). A keyboard appears and you can type your message. Tap the X icon to clear that custom message and return to the previous default reply.

Now your new message will be in the list when you reply to a text on your watch (**Figure 4.26**).

Figure 4.25 Tap and type in a custom reply.

Figure 4.26 And now the custom reply appears on the list.

The kids, they like the emoji. Emoji are the little pictures that started off in Japan and now everyone uses to text each other. Your watch, of course, can text emoji in addition to text. In fact, there's a dedicated emoji button (**Figure 4.27**). Tap that button in any text message reply and you'll be able to choose to send from two different sets of emoji: the standard set that is on your iPhone, and a new animated list of emoji that Apple designed just for Apple Watch.

Figure 4.27 The emoji icon.

To send an animated emoji response:

1. Tap Reply, which takes you to the text composition screen.

2. Tap the emoji button.

3. The first option you'll see are animated faces. Swipe to see the other two animated options: hearts and hands (**Figure 4.28**). To scroll through the options, turn the Digital Crown and the animated emoji will change before your very eyes.

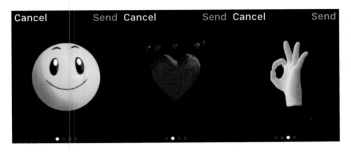

Figure 4.28 Three types of animated emoji: smiles, hearts, and hands.

The face and heart animated emoji have one additional option: color. Force touch the face emoji to change the color from yellow to red (force touch again to change back). The heart has three color options: red, blue, and pink. The gloved hand does not offer additional color options.

Once you settle on an animated emoji, tap Send and off it goes.

▶ **TIP** Animated emoji will animate by default when received on an Apple Watch. If the text is received on something other than an Apple Watch, it'll be sent as a picture, which may or may not animate depending on the device.

If the traditional emoji is more your speed, you can send them too:

1. Tap Reply, which takes you to the text composition screen.

2. Tap the emoji button.

3. Swipe until you're at the last emoji screen (**Figure 4.29**). Your recently used emoji (which is pulled from your iPhone) are listed first. Use the Digital Crown to scroll through the entire list of emoji until you find the one you want to send.

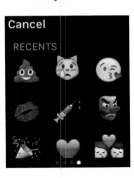

Figure 4.29 Traditional emoji are also an option, with your recently used on the first screen.

4. Tap the emoji you want to send and your Apple Watch sends it. Composing emoji sentences is impossible on your watch since you can't send more than one emoji at a time. Choose wisely.

Message list

You can also access your list of text messages on Apple Watch via the Messages app. To launch the Messages app:

1. Press the Digital Crown until you're on the Home screen and tap the Messages icon.

2. The list of text messages appears on your Apple Watch (**Figure 4.30**). This list matches the list on the paired iPhone. Use the Digital Crown to scroll through the list, and tap on any message to see the entire conversation (**Figure 4.31**).

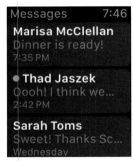

Figure 4.30 The list of your text messages. Unread messages have a blue dot next to them.

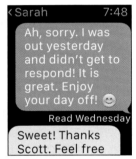

Figure 4.31 A text conversation. Your texts are displayed in blue.

In the list swipe right on a conversation to reveal the Details and Trash buttons (**Figure 4.32**). The Details button displays that contact's information. Tap the Trash button to remove the entire conversation from your watch (and your iPhone). A second Trash button appears to confirm that you really want to delete this conversation. Tap it, and the conversation is deleted forever (well, at least your side of the conversation is deleted; it could still be on the other person's devices).

Figure 4.32 Swipe on a conversation in the message list to reveal the Details and Trash buttons.

Force touching in the list of messages brings up the New Message button (**Figure 4.33**). Tap this and a slightly different text composition screen appears (**Figure 4.34**). This screen allows you to compose a message to anyone in your contacts. Tap the Contacts button and you'll see a list of the people you most recently texted. Tap the Contact icon to select someone from your full list of contacts. Once you have the recipient selected, tap Create Message and you're given the usual options of the list of default replies, dictation, and emoji. Create your message and then tap Send to send it off to the recipient. This message is either created as a new conversation in the message list or added to an already existing conversation you've been having with the contact.

Figure 4.33 Force touch to bring up the New Message button.

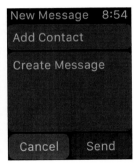

Figure 4.34 The new message screen.

Tap on a conversation to see all the messages in it. At the top of the conversation is the day and time that it started. This area also indicates whether this is an iMessage conversation or a text message conversation (**Figure 4.35**). Any pictures that you've been texted will be displayed in the appropriate conversations (**Figure 4.36**). Tap on the picture to see it full screen on the watch, and then tap on the upper left of the screen to go back to the conversation. If you swipe right, the message bubbles will slide to the side and reveal the time at which that message was received or sent (**Figure 4.37**).

Figure 4.35 An iMessage conversation. The pizza did arrive.

Figure 4.36 Texts with images are supported on Apple Watch. You can receive images but you can't send them from the watch.

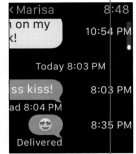

Figure 4.37 Swipe left in a conversation to see the time stamps for each message.

If you scroll all the way to the end of a conversation, a Reply button appears. Tap it to compose a new text message.

Force touching while you're in a conversation brings up three buttons: Reply, Details, and Send Location (**Figure 4.38**). Tapping Reply opens the text composition screen. Details takes you to that contact's details (scroll down to see all the information you have for that person) (**Figure 4.39**). Tapping Send Location will send this person a map with your location pinned into it (**Figure 4.40**). They can tap it to open it in their phone or watch's map app. You need to give Messages permission to determine your current location for Send Location to work.

Figure 4.38 Force touch in a conversation to bring up the Reply, Details, and Send Location buttons.

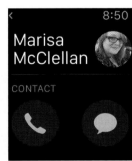

Figure 4.39 Tapping the Details button takes you to that person's contact.

Figure 4.40 Send Your Location sends a map with your location noted on it.

► **TIP** To send a text message to a number that isn't assigned to any of your contacts, use Siri. Press and hold the Digital Crown until the Siri screen appears. Say "Send a text message to…" and speak the phone number. Siri will think for a moment and then take you to the text composition screen. Create your message and when you tap Send it'll be sent to the number you dictated.

Failure to text

Sending text messages from your Apple Watch requires that your paired iPhone be within range. Sometimes, even when it is in range, a message will fail to send (**Figure 4.41**). Tap on the red exclamation point to bring up the Try Again button (**Figure 4.42**). Tap that and your watch will attempt to send the message again. If it fails, you'll be alerted and the exclamation point will remain beside the message in the list.

Figure 4.41 Sometimes a text fails to send. Tap the exclamation mark to resend.

Figure 4.42 Tap Try Again and the watch will attempt to resend the message.

Friends

Press the Side button on your Apple Watch and you're taken to the Friends screen (**Figure 4.43**). Since Apple decided to dedicate one of the few physical buttons on the watch to the Friends screen, you know it's important. This is how you initiate contact with the people you care most about via your watch. Think of this as the favorites on your iPhone, which in fact, is how the Friends screen is populated by default.

Figure 4.43 The Friends screen lists your favorite people.

When you first set up your watch, anyone you've marked as a favorite in your contacts will be listed on the Friends screen (if you have more than 12 favorites you're very popular, and only the first 12 will be listed on the Friends screen).

The Friends screen makes it very easy to text, call, and use Digital Touch (only with your friends who have an Apple Watch) with a couple of taps.

You can use the Digital Crown to select one of the 12 friends, or you can tap on one to select it. Then, tap on the middle circle to go to the Friends screen (**Figure 4.44**). You can call, use Digital Touch, or text the friend by tapping on one of the icons along the bottom of the screen.

Figure 4.44 The Friends detail screen gives you the option to call, use Digital Touch, and text.

Adding friends

As I mentioned, your favorite contacts are added to the Friends screen by default. You can add other people easily, though they must be in your iPhone's contacts first:

1. Launch the Apple Watch iPhone app and tap Friends.

2. The list of your current friends is displayed (**Figure 4.45**). To the left of your friend's name is an icon that depicts their location on the Friends screen circle. Tap the I in a circle icon to see that friend's contact information right in the Apple Watch app. Each slot that doesn't currently have a friend assigned to it simply displays Add Friend. Tap one.

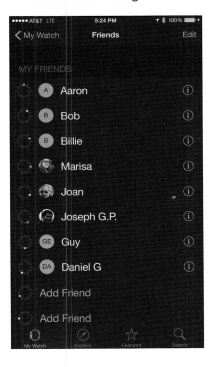

Figure 4.45 Manage your friends via the Apple Watch app.

3. The Contacts chooser appears (**Figure 4.46**). You can scroll through your contacts to find the friend you want to add, or search for them at the top the screen. Once you've found the contact you want to add as a friend, tap on it. Contacts that are already listed in your Friends screen are grayed out.

Figure 4.46 Pick a contact to add to your Friends screen.

That contact will now appear on your Friends list and will appear on your watch's Friends screen.

Friendly faces

You'll notice that some people have pictures displayed on their contacts in the Friends screen, while others are just initials in a circle. If a contact doesn't have a photo assigned to them in your iPhone, their Friends screen entry will be their initials.

To assign a picture to a contact:

1. Launch the Contacts app on your iPhone.

2. Find the contact you want to assign a picture to and tap on it.

3. Tap Edit to edit the contact.

4. Tap on the "add photo" circle next to the contact's name (**Figure 4.47**).

Figure 4.47
A contact's detail on the iPhone.

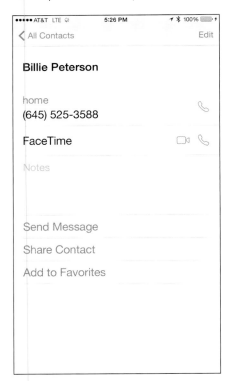

5. Three buttons appear: Take Photo, Choose Photo, and Cancel (**Figure 4.48**).

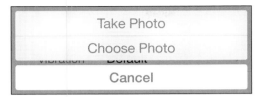

Figure 4.48 You can assign a new or existing photo to any of your contacts.

Take Photo allows you to use the iPhone's camera to take a picture that will be assigned to the contact. Tap this button, and then point the camera at whatever you want to take a picture of. Tap the white shutter button and a photo will be taken. The picture is previewed in a circle (**Figure 4.49**). Move and resize it with your fingers to fit best in the circle. When you're happy with it, tap Use Photo (tapping Retake allows you to take another photo).

Figure 4.49 When you take a new photo, it is masked by a circle so you can see how it'll be displayed.

The photo will now be assigned to that contact (**Figure 4.50**).

Figure 4.50 The photo assigned to Billie's contact.

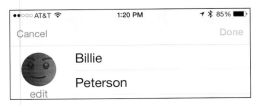

Tapping Choose Photo allows you to pick a picture already on your iPhone to go through the same process.

Tap Done on the contact and the photo will be assigned to this contact. After a few minutes, it will appear on the Friends screen on your Apple Watch as well.

Removing friends

With only 12 slots on the Friends screen you might need to move some friends out of the circle to make room for others. You can do this by swiping left across a friend in the Friends section of the Apple Watch app (**Figure 4.51**). This reveals a Remove button, which you can then tap to remove the friend from the Friends screen.

Figure 4.51 Swipe left on a friend to reveal the Remove button.

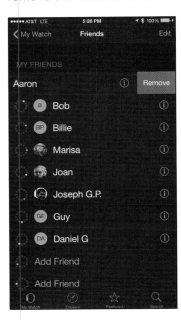

If you want to do a mass removal:

1. Launch the Apple Watch app and tap on Friends.

2. Tap Edit at the top right of the Friends screen.

3. Tap the circle next to each of the friends you want to delete and the Remove button will appear (**Figure 4.52**). Tap the circles next to the friends you want to remove until they are all removed from the Friends screen.

Figure 4.52 In the Edit mode, tap the minus icon to quickly delete friends.

If you want change the order of the Friends screen, you also do that in the Apple Watch app:

1. In the Friends section of the Apple Watch app, tap the Edit button at the top right of the screen.

2. On the right side of each friend slot there is a three-lined icon. Tap and drag on that icon to reorder the friends on the Friends screen. If you don't have 12 people to add to your Friends screen (I don't), I find it nice to use empty slots as spacers between each friend.

Interacting with friends

When a friend is selected in the Friends screen, up to three icons appear at the bottom of the screen: phone call, Digital Touch, and text message. Each of these interactions requires that the paired iPhone be in range, and Digital Touch requires that the person you're contacting also have an Apple Watch (more on what, exactly, a Digital Touch is in a moment).

Phone call

Calling anyone in your friends is pretty easy. Bob likes to make use of this feature when he is driving, since he can be on the phone without having the phone in his hand (since it is on his wrist!).

To call on of your friends from your wrist:

1. Press the Side button to go into the Friends screen.

2. Scroll or tap to select the friend you want to call and then tap on the center circle.

3. Tap the phone icon on the left of the screen.

4. If your friend has more than one phone number in their contact information, each is displayed (**Figure 4.53**). Tap on the number you want to call.

Figure 4.53 When a contact has more than one phone number, your watch displays the options.

Your friend's name will be displayed along with a message that says Calling Mobile (or whatever phone number you selected), and you'll hear the phone ringing.

Digital Touch

Digital Touch is strictly an Apple Watch–to–Apple Watch mode of communication, which takes three forms: sketches, taps, and heartbeats. Each of the three is sent directly to another Apple Watch, where they are displayed on the screen. Once you send another Digital Touch to that same person, it replaces the previous Digital Touch. This makes Digital Touches fleeting and ephemeral, but your watch does store the last received Digital Touch, which can be replayed until a new one is delivered that replaces it.

The Digital Touch icon appears under your friend in the Friends screen to indicate that they can receive Digital Touches (which also means that they, too, have an Apple Watch) (**Figure 4.54**). If the icon doesn't appear, that means you can't send that person a Digital Touch.

 Figure 4.54 The Digital Touch icon.

To initiate a Digital Touch:

1. Press the Side button to go to the Friends screen.

2. Select the friend you'd like to send a Digital Touch to, and tap them.

3. If the Digital Touch icon appears, tap it to enter the Digital Touch screen.

The Digital Touch screen is a blank canvas on which you draw, tap, or touch with two fingers to send one of the three supported Digital Touches: sketches, taps, or heartbeats (**Figure 4.55**). At the top of the left of the canvas is the recipient, on the right side is the color picker (more information in a moment), and at the bottom is a button that'll show you some more information about the ways you can use the canvas.

 **Figure 4.55** The Digital Touch screen.

Sketches, as you might guess, are little drawings that you sketch with your fingertip against the Apple Watch's display.

To send a sketch:

1. Press the Side button to go to the Friends screen, tap on the friend you want to send a sketch to, and then tap the Digital Touch button.

2. This takes you to the Digital Touch screen. Start sketching with your fingertip (**Figure 4.56**). As you sketch, your drawing appears. Once you're finished (the watch assumes you're done once you raise your finger off the display for a few seconds), the drawing seemingly fades from the display.

Figure 4.56 A sketch of a heart.

This fading means that the sketch has been sent to your contact.

When a sketch is received, it appears as if you're drawing the sketch on your friend's watch.

Taps bring haptics to the Digital Touch party. When you send a tap to someone's watch, it taps them on the wrist, much like an alert. Little color ripples are also displayed, as the watch taps the receiver in exactly the same spots that you tapped.

To send a tap:

1. Press the Side button to open the Friends screen and select the friend you want to tap. Tap the Digital Touch button.

2. On the Digital Touch screen, tap with your finger. Each time you tap the display, you'll feel a haptic touch on your wrist and the screen will display colorful ripples originating from your fingertip (**Figure 4.57**).

Figure 4.57 A tap on the Digital Touch screen causes colorful ripples.

The ripples fade away, and they are sent along to your Apple Watch–wearing friend.

When you're on the Digital Touch screen, you'll see a small colored circle in the upper-right corner. This determines the color of your sketches and the color of the ripples created by the taps. You can change this color to a few default options, or even select a custom color:

1. Tap the color circle to bring up the color picker (**Figure 4.58**).

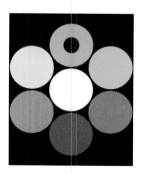

Figure 4.58 The color picker. The currently selected color is denoted by a black dot.

2. Tap one of the color circles to select it. A black dot will appear in the middle of the circle to denote your selection.

If you force touch on one of the colored circles in the picker, the custom color picker will appear (**Figure 4.59**). Drag your finger along the color wheel to pick a color and tap Done to select it.

Figure 4.59 The custom color picker.

The custom color will replace whatever color the circle was previously, and the new custom color will be selected.

The last kind of Digital Touch you can send uses the display, the haptic feedback, and the heart rate sensor to create something that is bit of a novelty (and a little creepy). You can send your heartbeat to any of your Apple Watch–wearing contacts. They will feel the beat of your heartbeat on their wrist, as Apple Watch taps it out in time to a stylized heart graphic (**Figure 4.60**).

Figure 4.60 Touch the Digital Touch screen with two fingers to send your heartbeat to someone.

To send your heartbeat to one of your contacts:

1. Press the Side button to bring up the Friends screen, select the friend, and tap the Digital Touch button.

2. Press two fingers to the Digital Touch screen. As you do this a heart graphic will appear; you'll feel taps on your wrist in time to your heartbeat.

3. Your heartbeat is recorded for as long as you hold your fingers against the screen. When you're satisfied with the length of time, remove your

fingers from the display and your heartbeat is sent off to your contact where it beats against their wrist (and they can respond in kind).

▶ **NOTE** Sometimes, for whatever reason, a Digital Touch will fail to send. A notification will be displayed with Retry and Discard buttons.

When you get a Digital Touch, your Apple Watch will notify you (**Figure 4.61**). The notification will include the type of Digital Touch, just in case you are in a meeting where it might not be appropriate to watch a little drawing on your wrist. You can dismiss the notification and play the Digital Touch later. Or you can tap the notification to be taken to the Digital Touch screen where the Digital Touch is displayed. You can then immediately respond with you own touch (or heartbeat).

Figure 4.61 A heartbeat notification gives you instructions on how to respond.

If you don't notice the notification, you'll also see a small blue dot next to the contact who has sent you a not-yet-watched Digital Touch in the Friends screen (**Figure 4.62**). Tap the friend and then the Digital Touch button to view it.

Figure 4.62 The blue dot means you have a Digital Touch waiting for you from that friend.

You can replay the last Digital Touch, and only the last Digital Touch, that someone sent to you by tapping the little play button in that contact's Digital Touch screen. Digital Touches aren't saved on the watch, or anywhere else for that matter, so enjoy them for what they are: ephemeral pieces of technology-mediated whimsy on your wrist.

▶ **NOTE** Any contacts that you've blocked on your iPhone will not be able to send you Digital Touches.

Texting a friend

The third button shown under a friend's detail is the text messaging button. Text messages, much like phone calls, come from your iPhone's number, so your friends won't need to add a special Apple Watch number to their contacts.

To send a text message from the Friends screen:

1. Press the Side button to go to the Friends screen and tap the friend you want to text.

2. Tap the Message button to bring up the text message options. The text composition screen appears. Choose either one of the default replies or an emoji, or dictate a message. See the "Text Messaging" section earlier for full details.

   The message is sent to your friend.

Presentations

Billie has a presentation to give at school, and her father taught her that walking around the room as you present is a good way to connect with your audience. However, she needs to tap the screen on her iPhone to advance her slides (Billie likes to do everything on her iPhone, so she runs all of her presentations from Keynote [$9.99 on the App Store: http://apple.co/1JSOQFN] or Microsoft PowerPoint [free on the App Store: http://apple.co/1bBFVtk] on her iPhone). Both Keynote and

PowerPoint have Apple Watch apps that act as remotes to control presentations, though the PowerPoint app is a little more full featured.

To use either remote app, you need to make sure you have either Keynote or PowerPoint installed on your iPhone. You'll also need the Remote watch app. To see if the Remote app is installed:

1. Launch the Apple Watch app on the paired iPhone.

2. Scroll until you see either Keynote or PowerPoint (depending on whichever app you want to use). Tap it.

3. Enable "Show App on Apple Watch" if it isn't enabled. If it is already enabled, that means the watch app is installed on your watch.

Both apps also require that the paired iPhone be connected to your Apple Watch. The iPhone doesn't need to be on a Wi-Fi network for it to work, but it needs to be within range of the watch or neither of the remote apps will be able to control the slideshows.

Controlling Keynote presentations

Keynote is Apple's presentation software, available on the Mac, iPhone, and iPad. The Apple Watch Remote app only controls slideshows being shown on an iPhone. If you're presenting from a Mac you'll need to use another solution (there is a Keynote Remote app for the iPhone that'll allow you to control the Mac app from your iPhone).

► **TIP** If you want to project a presentation from an iPhone, you'll need to pick up a VGA or HDMI adapter from Apple so you can connect your iPhone to a projector.

To use the Keynote Remote app on your watch:

1. Press the Digital Crown until you're in the Home screen and tap the Keynote icon (**Figure 4.63**).

 Figure 4.63 The Keynote Remote app icon.

2. Keynote launches and tells you to start a presentation on your iPhone (**Figure 4.64**). Once you launch a presentation on the iPhone, a play

button appears on the watch app with the name of your paired iPhone underneath (**Figure 4.65**).

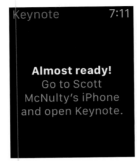

Figure 4.64 The Keynote Remote Watch app tells you to launch Keynote on your iPhone.

Figure 4.65 A large play button. Tap it to start your Keynote presentation.

3. Tap the green play button to start the presentation on the iPhone. A forward button appears, along with the total number of slides and the number of the slide you're currently on (**Figure 4.66**). Tap the forward button to advance the slide presentation.

Force touch to bring up two additional buttons: Back and Exit Slideshow (**Figure 4.67**). Tapping Back will take you to the previous slide and add a back button to the display of the Keynote remote (**Figure 4.68**). Now you can easily go forward and backward in the presentation.

Figure 4.66 The next slide button, with the current slide displayed below it.

Figure 4.67 Force touch to reveal the Back and Exit Slideshow buttons.

Figure 4.68 Force touch the Keynote Remote screen to display back and forward buttons.

Tapping Exit Slideshow exits the slideshow on the iPhone.

Controlling PowerPoint presentations

PowerPoint is the presentation app in Microsoft's Office Suite. It's available on the iPhone/iPad, Mac, and PC. Much like the Keynote Remote, the PowerPoint Apple Watch Remote will only control a PowerPoint presentation on the paired iPhone.

▶ **NOTE** PowerPoint on the iPhone is free as long as you only want to view presentations. If you want to edit/create presentations using PowerPoint on iOS, you'll need to purchase an Office 365 membership.

To use the remote with a PowerPoint presentation on your iPhone:

1. Press the Digital Crown until you're on the Home screen. Tap the PowerPoint icon to launch the app (**Figure 4.69**).

Figure 4.69 The PowerPoint Remote app icon.

2. A message tells you to open a presentation on the paired iPhone (**Figure 4.70**).

Figure 4.70 Much like the Keynote app, the PowerPoint Remote app needs you to launch Power-Point on your iPhone to function.

3. As soon as you open a presentation, the watch app displays an orange play button (**Figure 4.71**). Tap it to start the presentation on your iPhone.

Figure 4.71 Tap the play button to start your PowerPoint presentation on the iPhone.

4. The PowerPoint Remote does a few things differently than the Keynote Remote (**Figure 4.72**). First off, it displays a timer so you can get a feel for how long you've been talking. It also has a large forward button, which when tapped moves forward in the presentation, and a smaller back button. Your slide position is displayed at the bottom.

   Force touch to reveal two additional buttons: Restart and End Show (**Figure 4.73**). Restart starts the presentation over at the first slide and End Show ends the presentation.

Figure 4.72 The PowerPoint display time elapsed, a back and forward button, and the current slide.

Figure 4.73 Force touch to show the Restart and End Show buttons.

Grocery Shopping

Bob has to hit the supermarket on the way home from work, and he is armed with a shopping list. Mary and Bob use Wunderlist to keep a list of groceries that they can both add to and remove things from. Once Bob, or Mary, gets to the grocery store, they open the Wunderlist app on their iPhones and never forget an item.

Wunderlist has an iPhone app that includes a companion Apple Watch app that allows you to see your list of to-do items (or items on a grocery list) and mark them complete. Bob thinks it is much easier to glance at his wrist to see the next item on his shopping list and tap it to cross it off than it is to pull out his phone and do the same thing. And with the magic of Wunderlist, all of his to-do lists stay in sync across the web interface, iPhone, iPad, and Watch.

▶ **NOTE** Although this example is a shopping list, Wunderlist is a great to do app that can be used to track all sorts of lists, all of which you'll be able to access on your watch.

First things first. You'll need to create a Wunderlist account:

1. Go to https://www.wunderlist.com/ and click on "Create a free account" (**Figure 4.74**).

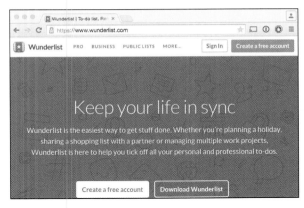

Figure 4.74 The Wunderlist website allows you to create a free account.

2. Enter your name, email address, and a password (**Figure 4.75**).

3. Click Create Free Account and that's it. You have a Wunderlist account.

Download the iPhone app on your phone and install the Watch App (Apple Watch App > Wunderlist > Show on Apple Watch). Launch the Wunderlist app on your iPhone and enter the account information you just created (**Figure 4.76**).

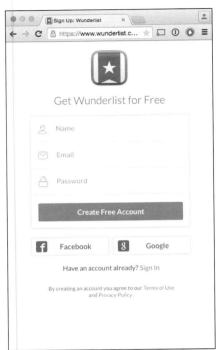

Figure 4.75 Enter a name, email, and password to create a free Wunderlist account.

Figure 4.76 The Wunderlist iPhone app login screen.

Bob has a shared to-do list with Mary in which they keep track of their groceries. To set up a similar list:

1. Launch the Wunderlist app on your iPhone.

2. Tap the Blue plus icon on the bottom of the app (**Figure 4.77**).

3. Two buttons appear: a green New List button and a blue New To-Do button (**Figure 4.78**). Tap the New List button.

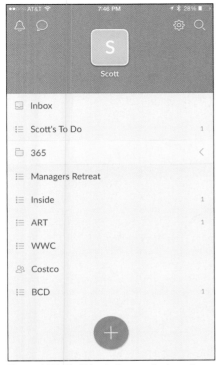

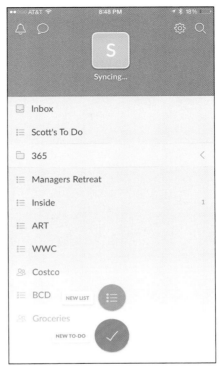

Figure 4.77 The Wunderlist app displays all your lists once you log in.

Figure 4.78 Tap the blue button to create a new to-do or the green button to create a new list.

4. Type in a name for your list (**Figure 4.79**) and tap Add People in the List Members section to invite someone else to share the list with you. If this is the first time you're doing this, Wunderlist will request access to your contacts. Tap OK and your list of contacts will appear (**Figure 4.80**). Scroll or search for the contact you want to share this list with and tap on the names to add them. Tap as many people as you'd like to share this list with. You may notice that some people in your contacts have a small red icon listed next to their email addresses in this list. This means that they already have a Wunderlist account.

   Once you've selected the people you'd like to share this list with, tap the Add button in the upper-right corner of the screen. They are added to the list members with a pending icon next to their name.

Figure 4.79 Give your new list a name.

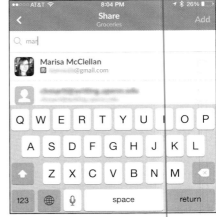

Figure 4.80 Invite any of your contacts to the list so they can add and remove things.

5. Tap the Create button in the upper-right corner to create the list. As soon as the list is created, an invitation will be sent to that person. If they have a Wunderlist account already, they will get an alert in the Wunderlist app in addition to an email. If they don't have an account, they'll be emailed with instructions to create an account with which they can access the list. You will be notified via email when the person you invited joins the list.

6. You're taken to the list where you can add things by typing them in and tapping either the Add button (at the top of the screen) or the Next button (on the keyboard) (**Figure 4.81**). Each item on the list can be starred by tapping the star icon next to it. This puts the item in a meta-list: Starred items (this will come up again in the Apple Watch app section).

Figure 4.81 Just type to add an item to a list.

Tapping on an item in the to-do list gives you a few options (**Figure 4.82**). You can add a comment or a due date, or assign the item to someone. Tapping the "Assign to" button lists all the people who have access to the list (**Figure 4.83**). Tap on someone to assign this task to them. Their initial is then displayed next to the task in the list.

▶ **NOTE** The Apple Watch app doesn't allow you to create lists or to add items to existing lists. Both of these things must be done either in the web interface or via the iPhone app.

Figure 4.82 Each item can be assigned to a person, a due date, a reminder, or even a subtask.

Figure 4.83 You can assign the item to anyone with whom this list is shared.

Once you have Wunderlist set up, and have a list with items on it, you can bring your Apple Watch in on the fun:

1. Make sure that the Wunderlist app is installed on your watch by going to the Apple Watch app on your iPhone, tapping Wunderlist, and then enabling "Show App on Apple Watch." The Wunderlist app also has a glance that you can enable once the app has been installed on your watch.

2. Press the Digital Crown on your Apple Watch until you're on the Home screen. Tap the Wunderlist icon to launch the app (**Figure 4.84**).

Figure 4.84 The Wunderlist Watch app icon.

3. The Wunderlist app displays four icons: Inbox (new items that aren't assigned to a list yet), Today (things with a due date of the current date), Starred, and Assigned To Me (**Figure 4.85**). Tapping any of these will list all the items across your lists that meet the criteria.

Figure 4.85 The Wunderlist gives you access to your inbox tasks, starred tasks, and things that are due and that are assigned to you.

Scroll down to see your full list of lists (**Figure 4.86**). Under the name of each list is an icon that indicates that it is just a list ▤ or a shared list ⚇ along with the number of incomplete items on the list. Tapping on any of the lists will display all the items with a box next to each (**Figure 4.87**).

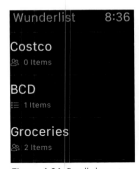

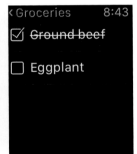

Figure 4.86 Scroll down to see the list of your lists. The number of items is displayed below the list name.

Figure 4.87 Tap a list to see the items on the list. Tap the box to complete the task.

As Bob throws things into his shopping cart, he taps the box next to it on his Apple Watch. It will be crossed out and then disappear.

The Wunderlist glance is pretty basic. When it is enabled, swipe up on the clock face and swipe until you see the Wunderlist glance (**Figure 4.88**). You might see a spinning circle while it loads items from the app. Once it is finished loading, any incomplete items that are assigned to you are listed. You can't check them off in the glance, but tapping on them takes you to the Wunderlist app, where you can interact with them.

Figure 4.88 The Wunderlist glance shows you the first incomplete task on a list.

Siri pictures

Whenever Bob is at the supermarket, Mary adds some sort of fruit or vegetable that he isn't familiar with. Who knows what a rutabaga looks like anyway? Siri on your Apple Watch does! You can ask Siri to find you some pictures of any number of things, including rutabagas:

1. Press in the Digital Crown to activate Siri.

2. Say "Show me pictures of *xx*" where *xx* is whatever you're after.

3. After a moment, Siri returns 10 pictures of the item in question retrieved from Bing Image Search (**Figure 4.89**). Use the Digital Crown to scroll down through the list. You can't save the images to your watch, and tapping on them doesn't do anything. But now Bob can identify rutabagas without looking foolish.

Figure 4.89 Siri can show you pictures from the Internet. These are rutabagas.

Apple Pay

Apple Pay allows you to pay for things in stores with your Apple Watch. It uses your existing credit card information to pay for things wirelessly in participating stores. You may already have Apple Pay set up on a supported iPhone, and if you do, you know how magical it seems. Hold your iPhone near the payment terminal, unlock the phone with your thumb, and the bill will be paid without you having to take out your credit card.

Apple Pay Security

Paying for things wirelessly certainly seems like something out of a science fiction movie, but people get nervous whenever you have to enter your credit card into something new. Apple Pay is probably a more secure way of paying for things than just using your credit card, for a few reasons.

First off, when you add a card to Apple Pay (see the instructions accompanying this sidebar) your credit card number isn't stored on the watch or on Apple's servers. Instead, during the activation process a unique *Device Account Number* is created and associated with your credit card/debit card. This number is not your credit card number, and it's stored locally on a special encrypted chip on the Apple Watch called the *Secure Element*. The Secure Element is the only place that this Device Account Number exists, and even if someone were able to get this number they couldn't charge anything to it. In order for a charge to go through with Apple Pay, the card's Device Account Number is needed plus a one-time security code that's generated dynamically at the time of transaction. The payment system and Apple Pay talk to each other, exchange those codes, and verify them, and then your charge goes through.

Why is this more secure than just swiping your credit card or debit card? When you use Apple Pay no one can glance at your card and perhaps write down the numbers to use them later. Plus, the store that you're buying things from has no record of your credit card; they just know that combination of the Device Account Number and the generated security code. This is significant if you think about all the times retailers have been in the news in regard to hackers gaining access to customer data. If the retailer doesn't have your credit card number, a nefarious hacker can't gain access to it.

To use Apple Pay on your watch, you'll need to enter a credit or debit card (if you want to use multiple credit cards, you'll have to set them up individually). Even if you have Apple Pay set up on your paired iPhone already, you still need to set up your Apple Watch. This ensures that you really want Apple Pay on your watch.

To set up Apple Pay on your Apple Watch:

1. Make sure the credit card you want to add to Apple Pay is supported. Most major credit cards from major banks are supported. This article has all the supported banks: https://support.apple.com/en-us/HT6288.

2. Once you have access to the card, launch the Apple Watch app on the paired iPhone and scroll until you see Passbook & Apple Pay. Tap on it.

3. As you can see by looking at the Cards section, Bob doesn't have any cards set up on his watch's Apple Pay just yet (**Figure 4.90**). Tap "Add Credit or Debit Card."

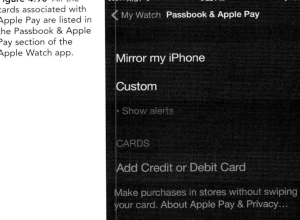

Figure 4.90 All the cards associated with Apple Pay are listed in the Passbook & Apple Pay section of the Apple Watch app.

4. You'll be asked for your Apple ID Password before you can proceed (**Figure 4.91**). This is to ensure that you are who you say you are and so Apple can look up the credit card they have on file with your Apple ID. Enter the password and tap OK.

5. Tap Next on the informational screen that pops up (**Figure 4.92**).

Figure 4.91 You must enter your Apple ID password to add a card to Apple Pay.

Figure 4.92 The first screen you see when you're adding a card has some information about Apple Pay.

6. If you have a credit card associated with your Apple ID (which is needed to buy apps, videos, music, or books via Apple's various digital store fronts) you can easily add that card to Apple Pay. You've logged in with your Apple ID, which Apple uses to retrieve that credit card information, and now you have to verify the security code on that card to add it (**Figure 4.93**). Once you do that, tap Next to add the card.

Figure 4.93 Apple cleverly offers to add whatever credit card you have on file with your iTunes account to Apple Pay first.

If you want to add a card other than the one you have on file with Apple, tap "Add a Different Credit or Debit Card." This takes you to the Add Card screen (**Figure 4.94**). You can use your iPhone's camera to automatically detect the numbers from the front of your credit or debit card. Just align the card with the frame on the screen and hold the phone steady. Your name, the account number, and expiration date will appear in white as the iPhone detects them (**Figure 4.95**).

Figure 4.94 The app allows you to scan a credit card with your iPhone's camera.

Figure 4.95 The camera reads your card's number and name. Of course, they won't be blurred out on your iPhone screen.

Next you need to enter the security code manually (**Figure 4.96**). While this use of the camera seems almost magical, and it is pretty accurate, double-check to make use all the information has been scanned correctly. If you notice an error, just tap on the field with the incorrect information and use the keyboard to correct it.

Enter the security code using the keypad and then tap the Next button in the upper right.

▶ **TIP** If you don't want to use the camera to scan a card, tap Enter Card Details Manually at the bottom of the scanning screen. That takes you directly to the screen where you can type in the card details using the keyboard.

7. An Adding Card screen displays (**Figure 4.97**). Wait for it to finish and then agree to the terms and conditions that appear by tapping Agree at the bottom right.

Figure 4.96 After the card information has been scanned, you have the opportunity to edit it and add the security code.

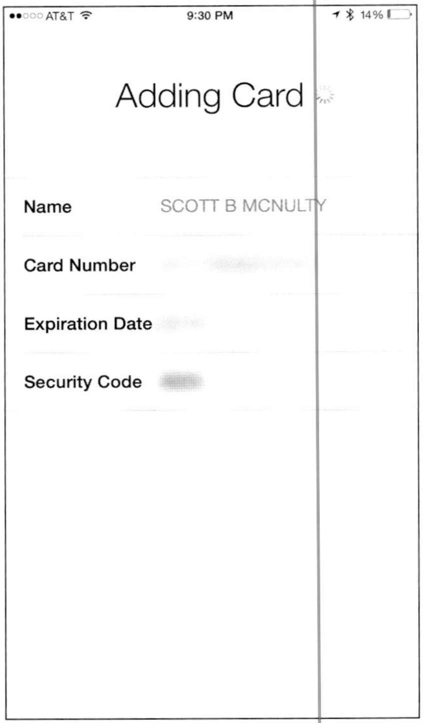

Figure 4.97 It will take a few moments to add the card.

8. You're taken back to the Passbook & Apple Pay screen, where the card you just added is displayed with Activating (in green) beside it. This means that Apple and your bank/credit card company are talking to each other, setting up the card to work via Apple Pay. Once the card has been activated, Activating no longer appears next to it. A notification appears on your watch alerting you to the fact that a card has been added to your watch's Passbook (**Figure 4.98**). You'll receive a notice from your credit card company, or bank, that your card has been added to an Apple Pay device. This is great, especially if you

haven't added a credit card to an Apple Pay device (in which case you should call your credit card company immediately).

You can add as many cards to Apple Pay as you like. Just tap "Add Credit or Debit Card" again to repeat the process.

Once a card has been added to Apple Pay, a new option appears: Default Card. If you have only one card in Apple Pay, that's the default card. If you have more than one card, tap here (**Figure 4.99**) to select the one you want to be automatically selected when you use Apple Pay (you can choose at the moment of purchase to use a card other than the default, but more on that later). The current default card has a blue check mark next to it. Tap a card to make it the default. When you do, the blue check mark appears next to it, and now when you use Apple Pay on your watch it'll use that card by default.

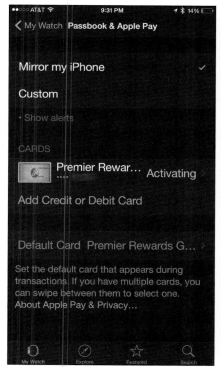

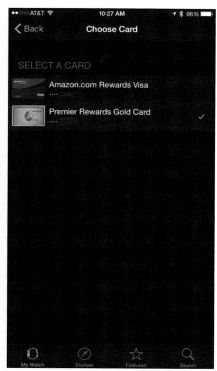

Figure 4.98 Now the card appears in the Cards section. It needs to activate before you can use it.

Figure 4.99 Tap on a card to set it as the default for Apple Pay on your watch.

▶ **NOTE** All of the settings discussed here only affect Apple Pay on your Apple Watch. Your Apple Pay setup on your iPhone, if you have it set up, is handled separately.

Using Apple Pay

You can use Apple Pay only at participating retailers. Most retailers that accept Apple Pay will display a logo that indicates Apple Pay is accepted near the point of sale (**Figure 4.100**). Apple also maintains a list of major retailers that accept Apple Pay: https://www.apple.com/apple-pay/where-to-use-apple-pay/.

Figure 4.100 The Apple Pay logo, displayed where Apple Pay is accepted.

▶ **NOTE** Apple Pay can also be used within apps on the iPhone, though not on the watch, so that isn't covered in this book.

Bob shops at Whole Foods, which just so happens to take Apple Pay. To pay for his groceries, Bob follows these steps:

1. He allows the cashier to scan all his items and waits until the final total is displayed on the payment terminal.

2. He raises his arm and presses his watch's Side button twice to activate Apple Pay (**Figure 4.101**). The watch displays the card that will be charged; this is the default card set in the previous section. Above the image of the card the word Ready appears, letting Bob know that Apple Pay is active.

Figure 4.101 The Apple Pay screen on a watch. Hold your watch near the reader to pay.

If Bob has more than one card in his Passbook, dots at the bottom of the screen indicate that there are more cards he can choose from. If Bob wants to use another card, he can swipe to change the card.

3. Once Bob has set the card he wants to use, he holds his Apple Watch near the payment terminal. His watch beeps and Bob gets haptic feedback once the terminal detects his watch and charges him through Apple Pay. When the charge is successful, a check will appear on the display and the register will spit out Bob's receipt (**Figure 4.102**).

Figure 4.102 The check mark, and a tap, lets you know the card was read.

A couple of things to keep in mind when you're paying with Apple Pay:

• If your Apple Watch isn't on your wrist, you'll need to enter your watch password before you can use Apple Pay.

• You might need to contort your wrist a bit to get your watch close enough to the payment terminal to make it work.

You can view all of the cards you have associated with Apple Pay on your watch by launching the Passbook app (press the Digital Crown until you're on the Home screen and tap the Passbook icon).

The Apple Pay cards are shown at the top of the list (**Figure 4.103**). Tap one to display it along with the instruction to press the Side button twice to activate Apple Pay. The only thing you can do with these cards in Passbook on your watch is view them like this. Force touching doesn't do anything.

Figure 4.103 Apple Pay cards displayed in Passbook on the watch.

Managing Apple Pay

All management of Apple Pay for your watch happens in the Apple Watch app on the paired iPhone. You can set custom notifications and remove cards via the app.

To set custom notifications:

1. Launch the Apple Watch app and tap Passbook & Apple Pay.

2. By default the notifications mirror those of your iPhone's. Tap Custom.

3. The only level of customization for alerts is either showing them or not showing them on your Apple Watch. Toggle to disable/enable them here. Keep in mind this setting only impacts your watch. If you want to change the notification settings on your iPhone, you'll need to do that through Settings > Notifications.

To remove a card from Apple on your watch:

1. Launch the Apple Watch app and tap Passbook & Apple Pay.

2. Tap the card that you want to remove (**Figure 4.104**). You'll need some information about the card, including the last four digits of the card and the Device Account Number (for more information about the Device Account Number, see the "Apple Pay Security" sidebar).

Figure 4.104 Card details in the Apple Watch app.

3. Scroll down until you see the Remove Card button at the bottom of the card information screen (**Figure 4.105**).

Figure 4.105 Tap Remove Card to remove the card from the Apple Watch's Apple Pay wallet.

4. Tap Remove Card and then tap Remove in the menu that appears.

   The card is removed and won't show up when you activate Apple Pay on your watch. If it is configured in Apple Pay on your iPhone, though, the card will still be available there.

Disabling Apple Pay on a lost or stolen Apple Watch

There may come a time when you lose your Apple Watch or it's stolen. That's a major bummer, but it's even more concerning if you have Apple Pay set up on the watch. Sure, it won't work unless someone knows your watch's passcode, but it's possible (though highly unlikely) that a thief could guess your passcode and have the ability to charge things with your watch.

You can disable a lost/stolen watch's ability to use Apple Pay remotely, and the best part is that the disabling process doesn't require the watch to have a data connection. Recall that when you add a card to Apple Pay you're prompted to enter your Apple ID password. This allows Apple to offer to automatically add the card you have associated with your Apple account to Apple Pay, but it also enables a link to iCloud. Now, none of your credit card numbers are stored on Apple's servers, but Apple's server acts as a go-between for your bank/credit card company and the retailer whenever you buy something. When this link is severed, Apple Pay for that card (or cards) no longer works. Since this link is associated with your Apple ID, you can manage it via iCloud in your browser.

▶ **NOTE** You'll need to know your Apple ID username and password in order to follow these instructions.

To remove all cards from Apple Pay on your watch via iCloud:

1. Go to www.icloud.com with your browser of choice (**Figure 4.106**).

Figure 4.106 The iCloud login screen. Log in with your Apple ID and password.

2. Enter your Apple ID and Password, and click the arrow next to the password.

3. After you log in, you'll see your iCloud Home (**Figure 4.107**). Here you can access the online versions of Pages, Numbers, and Keynote, as well as your calendar, iCloud email, and more. Click Settings.

Figure 4.107 Click Settings in the iCloud home screen.

4. The Settings page has links to manage your Apple ID and change the language you use on iCloud, and also displays your iCloud storage amounts (**Figure 4.108**). The section we're interested in, however, is the My Devices section.

My Devices lists all the devices that are associated with the Apple ID you used to log into iCloud. Devices that have Apple Pay configured on them are denoted with a small Apple Pay logo ⬛Pay. Your Apple Watch should be on this list, assuming you logged in with the same Apple ID as the one you use with the paired iPhone and that you used to set up Apple Pay.

Click on your watch in the My Devices section.

Figure 4.108 All the devices associated with this Apple ID are displayed. Any that have Apple Pay enabled have a little Apple Pay icon.

5. Some details about your Apple Watch are displayed, including the last 5 digits of its serial number (**Figure 4.109**). More relevant to this section, any cards that you have set up in Apple Pay on the watch are displayed by their name and with the last few digits of the card number. There's also a Remove All link displayed underneath them. To remove all the cards from Apple Pay on this watch, click that link.

Figure 4.109 Click on a device to see some more details and the Remove All link.

6. An alert appears explaining that you're about to remove all the cards from Apple Pay on this device (**Figure 4.110**). If you're sure, click Remove and the removal process starts. It may take a few minutes for the cards to be removed from your Apple Watch. Apple will send you an email confirming that the cards have been removed and can no longer be used with Apple Pay on that watch unless you readd them.

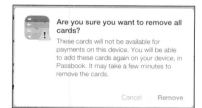

Figure 4.110 A warning, just in case you don't want to remove all the cards from Apple Pay on this device.

If you try to use Apple Pay on your watch during the removal process, you'll get an error message explaining that the cards are being updated and you can't use Apple Pay during the update process (**Figure 4.111**).

Figure 4.111 If you try to launch Apple Pay on the watch during this process, you'll see this error.

Once the process is complete, you can still launch Apple Pay and see the cards on the screen, but a Card Unavailable message is displayed above the card (**Figure 4.112**). If you open the Apple Watch app on the paired iPhone and tap Passbook & Apple Pay, you'll see that each of the cards is listed as Unavailable as well.

Figure 4.112 After the cards have been removed, they can't be used on your Apple Watch until you readd them.

Tap each one to remove them from the Apple Watch app. If the paired Apple Watch is in range, the cards will be removed from it as well. If it isn't in range, the cards will still show up but they can't be used.

If you recover your Apple Watch, you can always readd any of the cards removed via this method just as if you were adding a new card to Apple Pay.

Ping Your iPhone

The afternoon is over, and Billie and Aaron are home from school. Aaron walks through the house, puts his book bag down, grabs a snack, and sits on the couch to watch some TV. He reaches into his pocket to check his phone and he realizes that it isn't there. Glancing at his watch, he sees that it is still connected to his iPhone, so it has to be somewhere in the house (Aaron has his phone automatically connect to the family's Wi-Fi).

Normally Aaron would retrace his steps and tear the house apart looking for his phone, but thanks to his parents the solution is right there on his wrist: his Apple Watch. Apple Watch can be used to cause the paired iPhone to make a repeated beeping so you can track it down.

To "ping" your iPhone from your Apple Watch:

1. Swipe up on the clock face to access your glances.

2. Swipe left until you're at the first glance: Settings (**Figure 4.113**). If the top of the glance says Connected in green with an iPhone icon, you can ping your iPhone.

Figure 4.113 The Settings glance is home to the Ping iPhone button.

3. Tap the bottom button with the icon of the iPhone making noise in it.

4. Your iPhone will make a noise, just once. Tap the Ping iPhone button to make the phone ping again and again until you locate it.

   If you tap and hold the Ping iPhone button down, it'll continue to ping as you look for it, and the iPhone's flash will go on and off. This is a big help if the iPhone has fallen under the couch or you're looking for it in a dark room. Just find the flashing light.

▶ **NOTE** Pinging the paired iPhone will cause it to make a sound even if it's muted.

CHAPTER 5

Evening

The day is winding down, and the Peterson family is headed home and then out on the town. Apple Watch doesn't get the evening off, helping with everything from getting directions, viewing boarding passes, and listening to music.

Maps

The Maps app on Apple Watch depends on the paired iPhone for both GPS and a data connection. If the iPhone is out of range, the Maps app won't be of much value to anyone. However, with the iPhone in range the Maps app is very helpful. Not only can you find your current location, but you can get walking and driving directions to businesses, addresses, and even arbitrary points on the maps.

To launch the Maps app, do one of the following:

- Swipe up from the clock face and swipe until you see the Maps glance (assuming it is enabled, which it is by default) (**Figure 5.1**). The glance displays your current location. Tap it to go to the Maps app.

Figure 5.1 The Maps glance shows you your current location.

- Press the Digital Crown until you're at the Home screen and tap the Maps icon to launch it (**Figure 5.2**).

Figure 5.2 The Maps Watch app icon.

Bob is supposed to meet Mary at a movie theater after work, but he isn't sure how to get there. He, of course, turns to his watch to help him out.

When you launch the Maps app, it'll determine your current location and put a blue dot on the map to indicate where you are. Use your finger and drag it against the display to move the map around. Use the Digital Crown to zoom in or out on the map. If you lose your location and don't know how to recenter the map on your location, tap the blue pointer icon.

Various points of interest will be displayed on the map with icons (a cross for hospitals, a bed for hotels, a tree for parks, and so on). Tap on one of those icons to see more information about that point of interest, including its address (**Figure 5.3**). From the Point Of Interest detail screen you can get walking or driving directions by tapping the appropriate buttons.

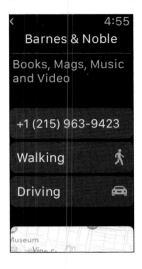

Figure 5.3 A location's details screen includes walking and driving buttons.

Force touching on the map brings up two buttons: Search and Contacts (**Figure 5.4**). Tapping on Contacts brings up the contacts picker. Tap on a contact and scroll down until you see a map with the contact's address under it. Tap this map and you're taken to another screen with the contact's name at the top and two buttons: walking and driving directions. Each button has the estimated time it'll take you to get to this address from your current location. Tap either to get directions.

Figure 5.4 Force
touch in the Maps app
to bring up the Search
and Contacts buttons.

Tap and hold on the map to drop a pin on an arbitrary location. You can
then tap on this pin to get directions to that point. This is useful if you're
parked in a large parking lot since you can drop a pin on your current location and then get directions back to your car. When it is time to return to
your car, tap the pin and then tap Walking Directions.

The Search button gives you three different ways to search for an address:

- **Dictation:** Tap this to use Siri to search for a location. You can tell Siri
  an exact address or ask for the nearest movie theater, which is what
  Bob does. When searching for a business (like a movie theater), Siri
  displays a list of results with star rankings pulled from Yelp displayed
  under the business name (**Figure 5.5**). Tap on one to get more details,
  including hours of operation and the business's phone number. Scroll
  down and you'll see the walking and driving directions buttons. Each
  button displays an estimated length of the trip, so you can get a
  sense for how long of a haul you're in for. Tapping either launches the
  directions.

Figure 5.5 Search
results include
Yelp ratings where
appropriate.

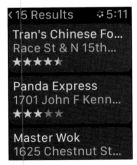

- **Favorites:** The Maps app on the iPhone allows you to save addresses to your Favorites list. Tapping this button on your Apple Watch brings up the Favorites list from your iPhone.

  To add a location to your favorites on your iPhone:

  1. Launch the Maps app on your iPhone.

  2. Search for an address.

  3. A pin will drop onto the map with a flag that shows the estimated driving time to that location (**Figure 5.6**). Tap on the flag.

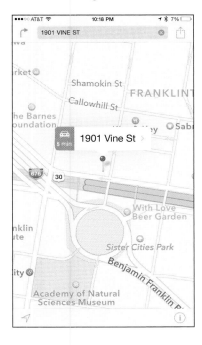

Figure 5.6 A pin dropped on a map includes a driving directions button.

  4. The location details screen has the full address as well as buttons for you to create a new contact with this address. Tap the Actions button in the top right of the screen.

5. The Actions menu appears with an "Add to Favorites" button (**Figure 5.7**). Tap it and the address is added to your Maps Favorites list. Now it'll show up on the Favorites list on your Apple Watch.

Figure 5.7 Tap the Actions button to reveal a menu so that you can add this location to your Favorites list.

- **Recent Addresses:** Any addresses that you've recently searched for on the Maps app on either Apple Watch or the iPhone will show up here. Tap to get the driving and walking direction buttons.

▶ **NOTE** Walking directions ignore things like one-way streets and the like, since pedestrians don't need to obey those traffic laws. The way you interact with each set of directions is the same, though. Be sure to select the right kind of directions.

The route is displayed on a map with your starting point indicated by a green pin and your destination by a red pin. Clear and Start buttons appear underneath the map, and you can zoom in and pan around the map if you like (**Figure 5.8**).

Figure 5.8 Maps will give you a route preview and an estimated time of arrival (ETA). Tap Start to see the turn-by-turn directions.

Tap Start when you're ready to go, and the instructions will appear on your watch face (**Figure 5.9**). The instructions screen includes the distance to the next turn, along with the directions for you to follow and an icon indicating which way you should go. At the top of the display you'll see your ETA. Tap on that time, and your watch displays the time it will take you to reach your destination. When you're following driving directions, highway and interstate signs will be displayed here when relevant (**Figure 5.10**).

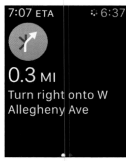

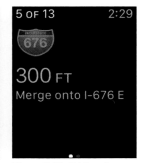

Figure 5.9 Instructions appear on the watch screen, and your watch taps you when a turn is coming up.

Figure 5.10 Driving directions will include highway and interstate signs.

Swipe up on the directions screen to see the next step in the directions. You can keep swiping up to look through all the steps ahead of time, so you can familiarize yourself with the route. As you're swiping through the steps, its number is displayed on the top left of the screen, so you can keep track of where you are in the directions. Tap here to return to the current direction you should be following.

Tap or swipe on the current direction screen to see your location on your route plotted on the map (**Figure 5.11**). You can swipe/tap back and forth between the two views as often as you like.

Figure 5.11 Swipe to see your current location on the route.

Apple Watch does not provide spoken turn-by-turn directions. Instead, the watch uses haptic feedback. When you need to make a turn, Apple Watch will tap you on the wrist using two distinct patterns:

- Left turn pattern: Three pairs of two taps
- Right turn pattern: 12 taps in a row

The screen will also display turning instructions. When Apple Watch is providing directions to you, it'll always be the screen that appears when you lift your wrist. You can switch to other apps and screens while using directions and return right where you left off without any trouble.

As you approach your destination, your watch will buzz and show you the remaining distance. Once you arrive, your watch will buzz once more to let you know you're in the right place (**Figure 5.12**).

Figure 5.12 Hurrah! You've arrived where you were going. Apple Watch celebrates by tapping you on the wrist.

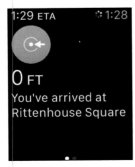

The map and directions are also displayed on the paired iPhone's lock screen in case you want to see more detail (**Figure 5.13**). If you unlock the phone, Apple Watch will hand off the directions to the iPhone and you'll hear spoken directions. Lock the phone and the directions are back on your Apple Watch.

Figure 5.13 Directions are displayed on your iPhone's lock screen when you're using the watch for directions.

Transit directions

The Maps app on the Apple Watch has you covered with walking and driving directions, but if you're in an urban environment and you're hoping for some public transportation directions, Maps can't help you. However, there's a great third-party app called Transit (free; http://apple.co/1zUAqle) that can help (**Figure 5.14**).

Figure 5.14 The Transit iPhone app icon.

► **NOTE** Transit currently works in over 90 cities; see http://transitapp.com/regions.

You must have Transit installed on the paired iPhone and then install it on your Apple Watch. The focus of the app is slightly different from that of the Maps app. In the Maps app you can get directions by entering your location and then your destination, and you'll get instructions to get there. You can do this via the Transit app on your iPhone, but the Apple Watch app concentrates on doing three things:

- Displaying the next available train/bus/other public transportation option that is near your current location

- Providing one-tap transit directions from your current location to home

- Displaying the last itinerary you searched for on your iPhone

When you launch Transit on your watch (go to the Home screen and tap the Transit icon), it determines your location and shows you the departure times of nearby public transportation options (**Figure 5.15**). The name/number of the route is displayed, along with the destination and the location where you can catch the train/bus. Under that information are the next three scheduled departure times.

Figure 5.15 The Transit Watch app shows you the next three leaving buses/trains near you.

Each bus and train line has two directions that it goes in, and you can get times and pickup locations for the opposite route by tapping on any of the items in the list.

At the top of the screen is a Home icon. Tap on this and you'll be told to set a home location in the iPhone app, if you haven't already.

To set a home location in Transit on your iPhone:

1. Launch Transit on the paired iPhone.

2. Tap in the "Search Line or Location" field (**Figure 5.16**).

Figure 5.16 Search for a location on the iPhone app to set a home address on the Transit app.

3. Type in your home address and Transit will list suggested addresses.

4. Tap and hold on your home address. Tap "Set as Home" in the menu that appears (**Figure 5.17**).

Figure 5.17 Tap and hold on a suggestion to set that as your home address. That isn't the author's home address.

Back on the Apple Watch, if you tap the Take Me Home button Transit will search all nearby public transportation options and display an itinerary that'll get you home (**Figure 5.18**). Use your finger or the Digital Crown to scroll through the directions. Tapping on any of the individual steps will take you to a map of the location mentioned. You can use the Maps app to give you walking/driving directions to the pickup location and then follow Transit's literary to get you to your destination.

Figure 5.18 An itinerary on the Transit watch app.

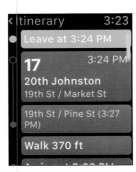

Finally, you can't search for a route with arbitrary start and end points on your watch, but you can view the directions from your last iPhone search on your watch. Just run a search on the iPhone in Transit and view the directions. Then launch the Apple Watch app and tap the Last Itinerary button ![ ]. You'll then see the instructions listed.

Going to a Movie

When going to a movie theater, you can do a few things to make sure your Apple Watch doesn't ruin the experience for you or others. As you know, when you move your arm the display of the Apple Watch turns on so you can see the time or whatever app you're currently using. Generally this isn't a problem, unless you're fidgeting in a very dark room with a bunch of strangers attempting to pay attention to the latest Hollywood blockbuster or indie sensation. The sudden appearance of your glowing Apple Watch face might not be widely appreciated.

Turn off your watch

The surest way to be certain that your watch doesn't disturb anyone is to simply turn it off while you're at the movies. You shouldn't be checking your watch anyway!

To turn off your Apple Watch:

1. Press and hold the Side button.

2. A menu with three options appears on the display (**Figure 5.19**). Slide the Power Off button to the right, and your Apple Watch will turn off.

Figure 5.19 Slide the Power Off button to turn off your Apple Watch.

To turn your Apple Watch back on, hold in the Side button until the Apple logo appears. After a few moments the watch will boot up (you'll need to enter your password again to access it).

Mute alerts

As you wear your Apple Watch more and more, there is a chance that you'll forget it is even on your wrist. This could lead to you being in a situation where it starts to make an alert sound and you want to stop that sound but not act on the alert. For example, Bob has settled in next to Mary in the theater and the trailers are rolling. He's silenced his phone, as the movie theater suggested, but neglected to turn off his Apple Watch. Billie calls Bob, and though his phone just buzzes, his watch plays the call sound.

Luckily Bob has enabled "Cover to Mute" on his Apple Watch. All he has to do to mute the call ringtone without answering the phone, or even raising the watch, is simply cover the Apple Watch display with his palm for 3 seconds. A tap will confirm that the watch is muted and whatever alert sound that was playing will immediately be muted. (You can hope that no one else in the movie theater noticed.)

To enable "Cover to Mute" on your watch:

1. Launch the Apple Watch app on the paired iPhone and tap Sounds & Haptics.

2. Scroll until you see the "Cover to Mute" option and toggle it on (**Figure 5.20**).

Figure 5.20 The Sounds & Haptics section of the Apple Watch app allows you to enable "Cover to Mute."

"Cover to Mute" is one of three ways that you can mute sound on your watch:

- On your watch you can enable mute by swiping up on the clock face to bring up the glances. Swipe until you're in the Settings glance and tap the mute icon (**Figure 5.21**). The icon will turn red to indicate that Silent Mode is on.

Figure 5.21 The Mute icon turns red (or pink?) when the watch is muted.

- Launch the Apple Watch app on the paired iPhone and tap Sounds & Haptics. Toggle on Mute (see Figure 5.20). This will also turn the mute icon in the Setting glance red.

To unmute either, tap the mute icon in the Settings glance or toggle off mute in the Apple Watch app.

When your Apple Watch is muted, you will still be alerted to notifications with haptics. Also, keep in mind that mute does not affect any timers or alarms that you may have set. When they expire or go off, you'll hear an audible alert even if your watch is muted.

Do Not Disturb

Mute effectively silences your watch, but what if you don't even want to be notified about alerts at all, not even with a tap on the wrist? Do Not Disturb is the answer. Notifications will still come to your Apple Watch (assuming you aren't actively using your iPhone, in which case the notifications will show up on the phone), but they will be logged so you can review them later.

To turn on Do Not Disturb on your watch:

1. Swipe up on the clock face to bring up the glances.

2. Swipe until you're on the Settings glance and tap the Do Not Disturb icon (it looks like a crescent moon) (**Figure 5.22**).

Figure 5.22 Do Not Disturb mutes all alerts. It turns purple when active in the Settings glance.

Do Not Disturb is now enabled on your watch. A small blue moon icon is displayed on the watch face to remind you that Do Not Disturb is enabled (**Figure 5.23**).

Figure 5.23 A moon icon appears at the top of the watch face to indicate Do Not Disturb is enabled.

To turn off Do Not Disturb, go to the Settings glance and tap the Do Not Disturb icon.

Do Not Disturb is also available on the iPhone. You can set your watch to mirror your iPhone's Do Not Disturb setting, and vice versa, to ensure that you won't be alerted to notifications on either your phone or your watch with one tap.

To do this:

1. Launch the Apple Watch app on the paired iPhone.

2. Tap Do Not Disturb and enable Mirror iPhone.

Now when you set your watch to Do Not Disturb the paired iPhone will also go into Do Not Disturb, and vice versa. If you want your devices to have independent Do Not Disturb settings, toggle Mirror iPhone off in the Apple Watch app.

When Do Not Disturb mirroring is enabled, you can take advantage of some settings that are controlled through the iPhone settings. The Do Not Disturb settings are found on the paired iPhone in Settings > Do Not Disturb (**Figure 5.24**).

Figure 5.24 The Do Not Disturb settings can be modified on your iPhone.

The first setting is simply a manual toggle to turn Do Not Disturb on and off from the settings. Below that you can set a schedule for Do Not Disturb to turn off. Tap Schedule to select a start and stop time for "quiet time" (**Figure 5.25**). During the specified time your iPhone and watch will enter Do Not Disturb without you having to lift a finger. You can manually turn off Do Not Disturb during this time.

Figure 5.25 Set this schedule and you'll never be disturbed between 4:16 and 4:25 p.m.

By default your iPhone and watch will alert you of phone calls only from people marked as Favorites in your contacts when Do Not Disturb is enabled. To change this, tap Allow Calls From in the Do Not Disturb setting and tap Everyone (all calls will alert you), No One (no calls get through), or Favorites (**Figure 5.26**). You can also opt to allow calls from groups you set in the iPhone contacts app.

Figure 5.26 Allow Calls From will alert you when someone in a particular contact group calls you.

Do Not Disturb will also, by default, alert you when someone calls you more than once in a 3-minute period, since this indicates that person really needs to talk to you. Tap this setting to toggle it off.

The final setting, Silence, only applies to your iPhone. By default, Do Not Disturb only silences alerts on your phone when it is locked. This doesn't impact Do Not Disturb on your watch at all.

Power Reserve

If you don't want to turn your watch off completely but you want to be certain that you won't get any alerts whatsoever, not even from those people who can bypass Do Not Disturb, you can use Power Reserve mode.

As the name implies, this mode is designed to extend your Apple Watch's battery by turning off every feature except the clock. This means that you won't be able to use any apps or, more importantly, receive any notifications or alerts on your watch. You will, however, be able to check the time when you raise your wrist.

There are two ways to activate Power Reserve mode. Here's the first:

1. Swipe up from the clock face to enter the glances.

2. Swipe until you see the Battery glance (**Figure 5.27**). Here you can see how much battery power your watch currently has alongside a graphic illustrating the same thing. At the bottom of the display is a button labeled Power Reserve.

Figure 5.27 The Battery glance tells you how much juice your watch has and allows you to start Power Reserve.

3. Tap the Power Reserve button and a little instructive text slides up, along with Cancel and Proceed buttons (**Figure 5.28**).

Figure 5.28 Before you enable Power Reserve, you have to know what it does. Tap Proceed to enable it.

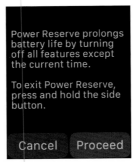

4. Tap Proceed and your watch immediately goes into Power Reserve. A digital time readout is the only thing displayed on the screen, and pressing/turning the Digital Crown or the Side button doesn't do anything.

Or you can do this:

1. Press the Side button in until three buttons appear.

2. Slide the Power Reserve button to the right. The watch enters Power Reserve mode immediately, without the warning that appears via the first method.

In Power Reserve mode, your watch won't alert you to anything, and it's not even connected to the paired iPhone (all of the wireless radios are turned off).

To exit Power Reserve mode, hold in the Side button until you see the Apple logo. You've just rebooted your watch into regular mode, so you'll get alerts once more. You also might have to enter your passcode.

Photos

Mary likes to have photos of her family on her at all times, because she's sentimental like that. Of course she has lots of photos of the fam on her iPhone, and a few in her wallet, but she doesn't want the watch to be left out of the party.

You can sync photo albums from your iPhone onto your watch. Once the photos are on your watch you can view them, and that's about it. The Photos app isn't very full featured, but you can use it to sync a photo of a pass you need to show to get into your building, or something like that, to avoid having to take out your iPhone or wallet.

To get photos onto the Photos app on your watch:

1. Launch the Apple Watch app on the paired iPhone and tap Photos.

2. The top of this screen deals with Photo notifications, which are mostly alerts (**Figure 5.29**). All of these alerts have to do with iCloud Photo sharing. If someone sends you a photo via iCloud, you'll get an alert. Tap Custom to disable this on your watch.

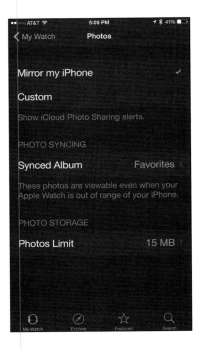

Below that is the section that determines what album of photos is synced with your watch. By default your favorites from your iPhone show up on your watch. Tap here to sync a different album (**Figure 5.30**). Tap on the album you want to sync and it'll start syncing, as long as the watch and the paired iPhone have an active connection. If the watch can't find the iPhone, the sync process waits until the connection is re-established.

Below that are the photo storage limits. You can set the limit to 25 photos (5 MB), 100 (15 MB), 250 (40 MB) or 500 (75 MB). The photos that appear on your watch are downsized from the iPhone; since the screen is so small, it doesn't make sense to send the full resolution. If you want to change the storage limit, just tap on one and the change is immediate.

▶ **NOTE** You'll get an error if you try to sync more photos than the limit allows.

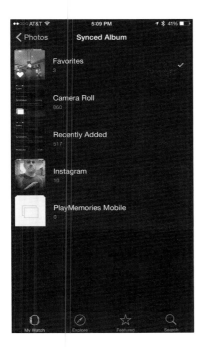

Figure 5.30 Tap an album to select it, and sync it to your watch.

Marking favorite photos on the iPhone

Mary doesn't want to send all of her photos on her iPhone to her watch; she just wants a selection of photos across albums. She could create a specific Apple Watch album and set that to sync with her watch, but there's another way that offers even more control: favorites.

By default the Apple Watch app only syncs photos marked as favorites in your photo roll on your iPhone. If you're like Mary, this means that your Apple Watch doesn't have any photos on it, but this is very easy to change.

To mark a photo on your iPhone as a favorite:

1. Launch the Photos app on your iPhone (**Figure 5.31**).

Figure 5.31 The Photos iPhone app icon.

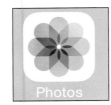

2. You'll see a list of all the photos you have on your iPhone (**Figure 5.32**). Tap on one.

Figure 5.32 Pictures in the Photos app.

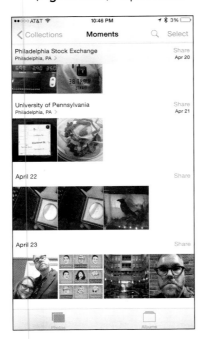

3. The photo will display on your iPhone (**Figure 5.33**). At the bottom of the photo are a few buttons. Tap the heart button to mark this photo as a favorite. The icon turns solid and the photo will be added to the Favorites album and synced to your Apple Watch (assuming that's the album you're syncing to your watch).

Figure 5.33 Tap the heart icon to mark a photo as a favorite. What a lovely-looking couple!

To remove favorite status from a photo, tap the favorite button again. The photo will be removed from the album and from your watch.

Viewing the photos

Now that Mary has some photos on her watch, she wants to view them. One of the nice things about syncing photos to your Apple Watch is that the syncing process creates copies of the photos on the Apple Watch's internal storage. This means that the paired iPhone doesn't need to be connected to the Apple Watch in order to view the photos synced to the watch (the iPhone can be turned off for all the Apple Watch Photo app cares, though the sync process requires the Apple Watch and iPhone to be connected).

To check the photos on an Apple Watch:

1. Press the Digital Crown until you are on the Home screen. Tap the Photos icon (**Figure 5.34**).

Figure 5.34 The Photos Watch app icon.

2. The only thing this app does is display pictures one by one. When it launches, the first picture in your album is displayed, blown up to be full display. Double-tap it to see the entire picture. Spin the Digital Crown to zoom in and out.

   Swipe to go to the next picture, and that's it.

The Photos app is pretty simple.

Taking photos

The Apple Watch does not have a camera, at least not version 1.0 of the hardware, so it may seem odd to talk about taking photos with it. However, the paired iPhone does have a camera and your Apple Watch can act as a remote shutter and viewfinder for your iPhone. Set your iPhone on a shelf, with the camera pointing at your family, run to join them, and then use your Apple Watch to take a picture with everyone in the shot.

▶ **NOTE** The Camera Remote app requires connectivity between the paired iPhone and the Apple Watch.

The app that allows you to do this is called the Camera Remote (**Figure 5.35**). To use it:

Figure 5.35 The Camera Remote app icon.

1. Press the Digital Crown until you're at the Home screen. Tap the Camera Remote icon to launch the app.

2. If the Camera app isn't open on your iPhone, tap Open Camera to launch it (**Figure 5.36**).

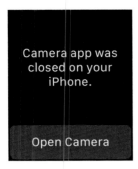

Figure 5.36 In order to use the Remote app, the Camera app on the iPhone has to be launched. Tap Open Camera to launch it from your watch.

3. The Camera app launches on the iPhone. The view through the camera is displayed on your Apple Watch along with two buttons: an immediate shutter button and a timer button (**Figure 5.37**).

Figure 5.37 The remote acts as a viewfinder for the iPhone camera. Tap the shutter icon to take a picture.

Tap the timer button (on the right) to display a countdown on the watch. The flash on the iPhone flashes in sync with the timer so that everyone can be ready for the shot (**Figure 5.38**).

Figure 5.38 Tap the timer shutter and a countdown appears on the screen and a picture is taken after 3 seconds.

Tapping the shutter button takes a picture immediately. You can also do this by pressing the Side button. Holding either down will cause the iPhone to take a burst of photos, so you can make sure that you get the right one.

As you take photos, they appear in the lower-left corner of the screen on your Apple Watch (**Figure 5.39**). Tap there and you can swipe through all the photos you took with the Remote app during this session (**Figure 5.40**). Just like in the Photos app, you can zoom in by turning the Digital Crown but that's about it. Tap the Close button to return to the Remote app.

Figure 5.39 As you take pictures, they appear in the lower-left corner of the app.

Figure 5.40 Swipe to look through the photos taken with the Remote app.

If the Camera app on the iPhone is closed while the Camera Remote app on the watch remains open, it'll display a message saying the Camera app was closed along with a button you can tap to relaunch it on the iPhone remotely.

The Camera Remote app only allows you to take pictures with your iPhone. Starting a video capture is not supported at this time.

Music

While their parents are off at the movies, Billie and Aaron are relaxing at home and in the mood to listen to some of their music. Apple Watch can be used as a remote for the Music app on your iPhone, and it can store music locally. Since Apple Watch doesn't have a lot of internal storage, it can't store as much music as your iPhone, but the iPhone doesn't have to be in range to play back music stored locally on the watch.

Controlling music on your iPhone

The default mode for the Music app on your Apple Watch is a sort of remote for your music library on your iPhone. To launch the music app:

1. Press the Digital Crown until you're at the Home screen. Tap the Music app icon (**Figure 5.41**).

Figure 5.41 The Music app icon.

2. The Music app launches and connects to your iPhone's music library (**Figure 5.42**). Mirroring the Music app on the iPhone, you can see music sorted by artist or album, or just look at a list of songs. Playlists are also available.

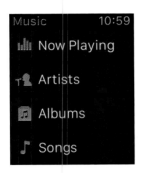

Figure 5.42 The Music app on the watch mirrors the sections in the iPhone app.

Tap on one; Billie tapped Album to see the list of available music (**Figure 5.43**). Tap on an album to see the song listing. In either list, use the Digital Crown to scroll.

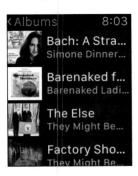

Figure 5.43 The Album list includes the cover, the name of the album, and the artist.

Tap a song to start playing it on your iPhone (**Figure 5.44**). As the song plays, controls appear on the watch's display. The song, album, and artist of the currently playing song are displayed at the top; the play controls (Back, Play, Forward) appear in the center and volume at the bottom. To adjust the volume, tap the plus/minus buttons or use the Digital Crown. Tap the display to show the album art of the currently playing song, and tap again to return to the controls.

Figure 5.44 The play controls include a play/pause button, rewind and fast forward, and volume controls.

Tap the play button to pause; tap it again to resume playing.

To return to the album listing, tap the top left of the display. If the currently playing song is in the list that you're currently viewing (which it is in this case), a special icon denotes this (**Figure 5.45**).

Figure 5.45 The currently playing song is denoted with an icon in the track list.

No matter where you are in the interface of the Music remote on the watch, you can always get to the currently playing song by force touching the screen (**Figure 5.46**). Depending on which screen you're currently on, you'll see a few options but one that is always available is Now Playing. Tap it to go to the currently playing song with play controls.

Figure 5.46 Force touch to gain access to the Source and Now Playing buttons.

The rest of the force touch options, and which screens they appear on, are as follows:

- **Source:** This is the other button that appears whenever you force touch the screen in the Music app. The next section will cover what this button does.

- **Shuffle All:** When you're in any list of songs (an artist's listing, an album, the song list, or a playlist) the Shuffle All button appears when you force touch the screen. Tap this button and all the songs on the current list will play in random order.

- **Repeat:** Force touching on the Now Playing screen reveals the Repeat button. Tap it to see the three repeat options: Repeat Off, Repeat Song, and Repeat All (which repeats the entire currently playing album or playlist). Tap whichever repeat option you would like.

- **AirPlay:** AirPlay lets you stream music from one Apple device to another (like from your Mac to an Apple TV). When the AirPlay button is tapped (on the force touch menu of the Now Playing screen), a list of all AirPlay-compatible devices that your Apple Watch can see is displayed. IPhone will be selected, since the music is currently playing on an iPhone, but tap any of the other entries to connect to them and stream the currently playing song to it. The controls function just as they do when you're controlling music on the iPhone via Apple Watch. If, for some reason, an AirPlay connect can't be made, an error message will display. Tap the AirPlay button again and tap iPhone to have the music play on the iPhone again.

iTunes Radio

iTunes Radio is Apple's advertising supported music streaming service (iTunes Match subscribers get to listen to iTunes Radio without ads). You can set up stations to play music or use some of Apple's stations.

Billie loves listening to iTunes Radio on her iPhone, and she wants to listen to it on her Apple Watch. However, at the moment you can only launch iTunes Radio on your iPhone. The Music app on the watch will allow you to control iTunes Radio once it has been started on the paired iPhone.

To control iTunes Radio on your watch:

1. Launch the Music app on your iPhone and tap the iTunes Radio icon (**Figure 5.47**).

Figure 5.47 iTunes Radio on the iPhone is Apple's music streaming service.

2. Tap on a station to start playing music.

3. Launch the Music app on the watch and you'll see the song currently being played via iTunes Radio on the iPhone (**Figure 5.48**). Almost everything is the same, with the exception of the lack of a skip button. It is replaced by a Star button.

Figure 5.48 The controls look slightly different when you're controlling an iTunes Radio station.

Tap it to help iTunes Radio tune the station (**Figure 5.49**). Tapping Play More means you like the current song and want to hear more like it. Never Play makes sure you'll never hear this song on this station again. Wishlist adds the song to your iTunes App Store wish list so you can buy it from your phone or computer.

Figure 5.49 Tapping on the star reveals options to play more songs like the one you're listening to, never play that song again, or add it to a wish list so you can buy it via iTunes.

Music on your Apple Watch

Much like you can with photos, you can sync music to your Apple Watch for playback without a connected iPhone. Again, the limited storage capacity of the watch requires that you designate a playlist for syncing to your watch, instead of just moving over all your music.

To sync music to your watch:

1. If you have an existing playlist on your iPhone that you want to sync to your Apple Watch, skip to the next step. If you need to create a new

playlist, open the Music app on your iPhone and tap Playlists > New
Playlist (**Figure 5.50**).

Figure 5.50 The
Playlists screen of the
iPhone Music app.

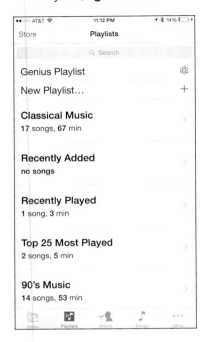

2. Enter a name for the playlist, and remember this name since you'll
    need to identify this playlist in the next steps (**Figure 5.51**).

Figure 5.51 Enter a
name for the playlist
you'll be syncing to
your watch.

3. Tap the plus sign next to the tracks you want to add to your playlist (**Figure 5.52**). Once you've finished, tap Done.

Figure 5.52 Tap the plus icon to add songs to the playlist.

4. Launch the Apple Watch app and tap Music.

5. The Music Syncing section displays the current playlist, if any, that is being synced to your Apple Watch (**Figure 5.53**). Only one playlist can be synced to the Apple Watch. When you change the existing synced playlist to another, all the music is deleted from your Apple Watch and replaced with the songs on the new synced playlist.

Tap Synced Playlist.

6. All of the playlists on your iPhone will be displayed, with the currently synced playlist denoted with a check mark (**Figure 5.54**). Tap the playlist you want to sync.

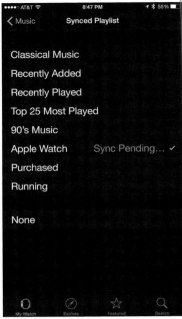

Figure 5.53 Set the synced playlist and limit on the Apple Watch app.

Figure 5.54 Once you select a synced playlist, the sync will be pending until you charge the watch.

7. "Sync Pending" will appear next to the newly selected playlist. The music will not sync until you place your Apple Watch on its charging cable. Once the iPhone detects that the watch is charging, the sync process begins. You can take your watch off the charger before the sync is complete, but that will pause the syncing process.

You can watch the sync progress in the Apple Watch app. Once the syncing is done, the music will be stored locally on your watch.

The amount of music you can transfer to your Apple Watch is limited, but you can customize the limits. Tap Playlist Limit to see your limit options (**Figure 5.55**). At the top you can select to limit either by storage amount (100 MB, 500 MB, 1 GB, 2 GB) or songs (15, 50, 125, 250). Tap to select which type of limit you'd like and then tap the value of the limit.

Figure 5.55 You can limit music based on song number or storage space.

Keep in mind that the syncing process is pretty slow, so the more music you allow, the longer it will take.

Once the syncing process is complete, you'll want to start rocking out to your sweet tunes on your watch. To play music that's stored on your watch:

1. Launch the Music app by tapping on it on the Home screen.

2. Force touch the display and tap the Source button.

3. A list of sources will appear: Apple Watch and iPhone (**Figure 5.56**). Tap Apple Watch.

Figure 5.56 Tapping the Source button presents a list of the available sources. Tap a source to control it with the app.

Apple Watch doesn't play music on its speaker, since that wouldn't sound very good. When you select the Apple Watch as a source, it prompts you to select some Bluetooth headphones to listen to your music through. Here's how to connect Bluetooth devices (including headphones) to your Apple Watch:

1. Make sure the Bluetooth headphones are turned on and in Discoverable mode (refer to the headphone's documentation for instructions on how to do that).

2. Press the Digital Crown until you're on the Home screen. Tap the Settings icon.

3. Tap Bluetooth (**Figure 5.57**). This tells your watch to scan for Bluetooth devices that are nearby. If your headphones are in Discoverable mode, they will show up in the Devices section after a few moments. Tap the headphones entry.

Figure 5.57 The Bluetooth settings on the Apple Watch.

4. After a moment the watch and the headphones pair (**Figure 5.58**). You can now use those headphones to listen to music stored on your watch.

Figure 5.58 Your watch will scan for available Bluetooth devices and list any the watch is connected to.

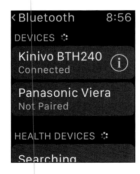

The headphones will show up as an AirPlay item in the AirPlay menu. This means that you can even use the Bluetooth headphones to listen to music from your iPhone controlled through your watch. Set

Source to iPhone and force touch the screen as a song is playing. Force Touch the screen and then tap AirPlay. Tap the Bluetooth headphones entry. Music will start playing through your headphones.

▶ **TIP** If you want to unpair a Bluetooth device, open Watch Settings > Bluetooth and tap on the connected device (**Figure 5.59**). Tap the Forget Device button and the devices are unpaired. To re-pair, follow the pairing instructions.

Figure 5.59 Tap on the device and you can unpair it from the watch.

Play Music using Siri

If you are more of a spoken word kind of person, you can play music using Siri. Hold the Digital Crown in to activate Siri. You can say things like

- "Play," which will start playing music in the Music app.

- "Play *artist/album name*," which will start playing all the songs by that artist or that are on the album.

- "Play *song name*," which will start playing that song. If you have two versions of the same song, Siri will ask you which one you want to play.

Siri will switch to the Music app, and the song/album you requested will play.

Music glance

The Music app also has a glance. To access it:

1. Swipe up from the clock face to access Glances.

2. Swipe until you see the Now Playing glance (**Figure 5.60**). You can start, pause, skip, and control the volume right from here. To open the

Music app from here, tap the top-left corner of the display. This will switch you to the full-featured Music app.

Figure 5.60 The Music glance.

This glance is very useful when you're out for a walk or run and you want to skip a track without pulling your iPhone out of your pocket.

The Music glance isn't limited to controlling the iPhone's Music app, iTunes Radio, or locally played music. If you're using an app like Spotify on your iPhone, the glance allows you to control it as well.

Remote

While their parents are off at the movie theater, the kids decide to rent a movie via their Apple TV. The Apple TV—Apple's streaming box that you attach to your TV and which allows you to rent/purchase media and stream your iTunes library to your TV—comes with a small remote...a remote that's very easy to misplace, and rather expensive to replace. Wouldn't it be grand if there was a remote for the Apple TV strapped to your wrist? Your Apple Watch can be used as a remote to control your Apple TV, and the chances of losing your watch are pretty slim.

First, you need to pair the Remote app to your Apple TV:

1. Be certain that the paired iPhone, and by extension your Apple Watch, are on the same network work at the Apple TV. The Remote app only works when you're on the same network with the Apple TV. To check which network your Apple TV is using, go to Settings > General > Network.

2. Once you've confirmed that you're on the same network, launch the Remote app by pressing the Digital Crown until you're on the Home screen. Tap the Remote icon (**Figure 5.61**).

Figure 5.61 The Remote Watch app icon.

3. Tap the Add Device button to add your Apple TV to this remote (**Figure 5.62**).

Figure 5.62 Tap the Add Device button to add either an iTunes library or Apple TV to the Remote app.

4. A code is displayed on the watch (**Figure 5.63**). You'll need to enter this code on your Apple TV to confirm the link.

Figure 5.63 A code is displayed on the watch, which you need to type into the device to complete the pairing.

5. With the code in mind, go to Settings > Remotes on your Apple TV (**Figure 5.64**). Your Apple Watch should be listed under iOS Remotes.

Figure 5.64 Under the Remotes settings on the Apple TV, the Apple Watch will show up.

6. Select your Apple Watch on the Apple TV and press the Select button on the remote.

7. Enter the code displayed on your watch into the Apple TV using the remote and press Done (**Figure 5.65**).

Figure 5.65 Enter the code into your Apple TV and press Done.

A link icon appears next to the Apple Watch on the Apple TV list. This means the Remote app has been successfully paired with the Apple TV.

You can also link the watch app to iTunes and control the playback of music on your Mac or PC. To do this:

1. Ensure that your watch is on the same network as the computer that has the iTunes library you'd like to control.

2. Launch the Remote app on the watch by pressing the Digital Crown until you're on the Home screen and then tapping the Remote icon.

3. Tap Add Device and a code will display on the screen, much like the Apple TV process.

4. Note the code and go to your computer.

5. Launch iTunes.

6. Right under the controls in iTunes is the Tab bar (**Figure 5.66**). There are icons for music, videos, and more. A new icon appears, the Remote icon, when you're attempting to pair a remote. Click on it.

Figure 5.66 The Remote icon appears in iTunes when you start to pair the Remote app to an iTunes library.

7. iTunes prompts you for the code displayed on your watch (**Figure 5.67**). Note that at the top of this window your Apple Watch's name is displayed. This is just in case multiple people are trying to set up a remote app at the same time for the same iTunes library. Enter the code.

Figure 5.67 Enter the code into iTunes to complete the pairing process.

8. Click OK on the confirmation screen, and now your iTunes library is ready to be controlled by your Apple Watch (**Figure 5.68**).

Figure 5.68 Success! You can now control iTunes with your watch. The future is here.

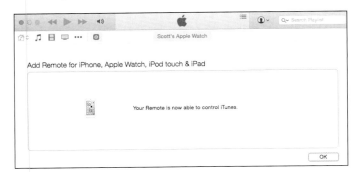

Using the Remote

Billie has paired her Apple Watch Remote with the family Apple TV (more than one person can pair remotes to an Apple TV, so there can be some remote fights), and her iTunes Library. When she launches the Remote, a list of the devices/libraries she can control is displayed (**Figure 5.69**). This list can be pruned by force touching on the screen. Two buttons appear: Add Device and Edit (**Figure 5.70**). Tap Edit and the device icons jiggle and an X appears at the upper-left corner of each (**Figure 5.71**). Tap the X on the device you want to remove and it will be removed. Tap the check mark in the upper right to exit editing mode.

Figure 5.69 Tap on the device you want to control.

Figure 5.70 Force touch to show the Add Device and Edit buttons.

Figure 5.71 In Edit mode the devices wiggle and have an X icon you can tap to delete the device.

▶ **TIP** You can control multiple Apple TVs and iTunes libraries with one Apple Watch remote app.

The Remote interface is slightly different when using it with an Apple TV compared to controlling an iTunes Library.

To control your Apple TV, launch the Remote app and tap on the Apple TV. The Apple TV Remote interface is pretty sparse (**Figure 5.72**). Swiping is very important in the Apple TV Remote interface. Swipe on the screen to move around the Apple TV interface. Swiping left will move the selector to the left, and swiping right moves it to the right, much like pressing left/right on the physical remote does.

Figure 5.72 The Apple TV remote screen depends on swiping to move the cursor around on the controlled Apple TV.

To select something, tap on the Apple Remote and the button on the Apple TV (the preview button on a video, for example) will be activated.

Once a video, or song, is playing, swiping left rewinds (swipe multiple times to speed up the process) and right fast-forwards. Tapping the screen pauses/plays the video. You can also tap the small pause/play button on the bottom right of the display to do the same thing.

To exit a video, or to move through the Apple TV menu system, tap the Menu button at the bottom left of the display.

To return to the device list in the Remote app, tap the button in the upper-left corner.

Tap an iTunes library on the device list and you'll see the iTunes Library controller (**Figure 5.73**). This interface looks very similar to that of the Music app, because it is pretty much the same thing though it is controlling playback on a computer and not the paired iPhone. The three buttons are

Skip Backward, Play/Pause, and Skip Forward. Spin the Digital Crown to turn up, or lower, the volume on the computer.

Figure 5.73 The iTunes remote screen has the traditional music controls, including volume.

You can have the music stream to any available AirPlay device on your network right from the Remote. Force touch the screen and the AirPlay button appears (**Figure 5.74**). Tap it and a list of available AirPlay devices appears (**Figure 5.75**). The device the music is currently playing out of is in light gray (Computer in this case). If other options are available, tap on one and after a moment the music will start playing out of that device. You can still control playback and volume from the remote. Force touch, tap AirPlay, and tap Computer to have the music play out of your computer once again.

Figure 5.74 Force touch to reveal the AirPlay button.

Figure 5.75 All devices capable of streaming music via AirPlay are listed. Tap a device to stream to it.

Travel

The Apple Watch is a perfect travel companion. It sits on your wrist, waiting to help you out whenever you need it, and you don't need to feel self-conscious pulling out your iPhone and looking like a tourist in foreign lands. Maps and Siri are great tools while you're in an unfamiliar city. Just say, "Hey, Siri, where is the nearest bookstore?" and then with a couple taps you'll get walking directions.

When you're crossing time zones you don't need to manually change your watch's time, which is nice. The Apple Watch automatically adjusts to the proper time zone and displays all of your appointments at the correct time.

Tickets

Mary has a flight to catch, and she hates printing out her boarding passes. Most major airlines, and Amtrak, offer Passbook versions of their boarding passes. Sadly, each airline does so in slightly different ways, but look for a button in the airline's app, or on the mobile boarding pass page, that says "Add to Passbook."

Why is this relevant? Because any boarding pass or train ticket that you add to Passbook isn't just available on your iPhone; it also appears in the Passbook on your Apple Watch automatically.

To display a boarding pass on your Apple Watch:

1. Press the Digital Crown until you're on the Home screen and tap the Passbook icon (**Figure 5.76**).

 Figure 5.76 The Passbook Apple Watch app icon.

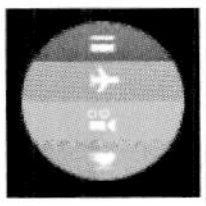

2. The boarding pass will be listed in Passbook. Tap on it.

3. The code the gate people need to scan is displayed on your watch. You might want to keep your iPhone handy, though, since the scanners at the gate weren't designed with scanning watches in mind. Your wrist might not fit under the scanner, so having the ticket on your iPhone is

a great backup. You don't want to miss your flight because the ticket couldn't be scanned!

Some airlines, including Delta, United, and American Airlines, offer dedicated Apple Watch apps. To install them, install the iOS app and the Apple Watch app will install along with it. All of these apps offer the following basic information on your wrist:

- Flight alerts for delays, gate changes, and more
- Flight status
- The baggage area where you should go to grab your bags

It is well worth checking to see if your airline offers an Apple Watch app before you fly.

Airplane mode

Once Mary manages to get on the plane, she needs to put her watch into Airplane mode. She can do so manually, or she can have her watch mirror her iPhone. When she puts the iPhone in Airplane mode, the watch will enter that mode as well.

To manually enter, or leave, Airplane mode on your watch:

1. Swipe up on the clock face to enter Glances.
2. Swipe until you're on the Settings glance (by default, it is the leftmost glance).
3. Tap the Airplane Mode button (**Figure 5.77**). It'll turn yellow and a message alerting to you the fact that your watch is disconnected from your iPhone will be displayed.

Figure 5.77 The icon turns yellow in the Settings glance when Airplane mode is on.

THE APPLE WATCH BOOK

If glances aren't your thing, there's another way to enable Airplane mode on the watch:

1. Press the Digital Crown until you're on the Home screen. Tap the Settings icon.

2. Scroll through the list until you see Airplane Mode (**Figure 5.78**). Tap on it.

Figure 5.78 Airplane mode has its own section in the Settings app.

3. Tap to enable Airplane mode (**Figure 5.79**).

Figure 5.79 Tap to enable/disable Airplane mode.

When your watch is in Airplane mode, a small airplane icon appears on its face (**Figure 5.80**). This shuts off all the wireless connectivity on your watch, meaning that even if your iPhone isn't in Airplane mode itself it will not be able to connect to the watch. All functionality that requires the paired iPhone will not work, but you can still see the time and your calendar, and look at locally stored photos. You will not be able to listen to any locally stored music on your Apple Watch while Airplane mode is enabled because that requires Bluetooth headphones and Bluetooth is disabled.

Figure 5.80 A small airplane icon is displayed at the top of the watch face when Airplane mode is enabled.

To turn Airplane mode off:

1. Press the Digital Crown until you're on the Home screen. Tap the Settings icon.

2. Scroll through the list until you see Airplane Mode. Tap on it.

3. Tap to disable Airplane mode. The Airplane icon disappears and your watch reconnects to the paired iPhone (if it's in range).

Or you can go to the Settings glance and tap the Airplane Mode button.

To mirror your iPhone's Airplane mode status on your watch:

1. Launch the Apple Watch app on the paired iPhone.

2. Tap Airplane Mode.

3. Tap Mirror iPhone (**Figure 5.81**).

Figure 5.81 With this setting enabled, turning Airplane mode on your Apple Watch enables it on your iPhone, and vice versa.

This mirror works both ways: when you enable Airplane mode on your iPhone the watch will also go into Airplane mode. When you put your watch into Airplane mode, the iPhone goes into it as well.

When you turn on Airplane mode on your iPhone for the first time after enabling mirroring, an alert will appear reminding you that your watch is also going to go into Airplane mode (**Figure 5.82**). Tap OK and now both are ready for flight.

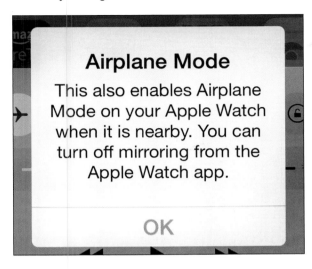

Figure 5.82 The first time you turn Airplane mode on after mirroring you get this warning. Heed it.

There is one thing to keep in mind when you mirror Airplane mode: turning on Airplane mode on either device turns it on for both, but turning off Airplane mode on a device turns it off *only* for that device. The mirrored Apple Watch will still be in Airplane mode until you manually turn it off. This makes sense because neither device can communicate with the other without wireless connectivity, which has all been turned off because of Airplane mode. Just be certain to turn off Airplane mode on both devices.

Getting a car

Mary's plane has landed, and now she wants to get to her hotel as quickly as she can. There's a huge line at the taxi stand, but Mary has the Uber app on her watch. Uber is a car service that you summon with a tap of a button. The service's iPhone and Apple Watch apps use GPS to locate you and route a car to pick you up. There is a slight premium as compared to taking a cab, but it is very convenient.

To use the Uber Apple Watch app, you'll need to install the Uber app (free, http://apple.co/1FiHni7) on your iPhone and sign up for an Uber account (with a credit card). When you're logged into that account and have the Apple Watch app installed, getting an Uber is simple:

1. Press the Digital Crown until you're on the Home screen and tap the Uber icon to launch the app (**Figure 5.83**).

Figure 5.83 The Uber app icon.

2. The Uber app determines where you are and displays one thing: a button with the estimated wait time for a car (**Figure 5.84**). Tap the button to call an Uber.

Figure 5.84 When you first launch the Uber app, it displays the estimated wait for a car. Tap the button to request one.

3. The location where you are standing is displayed as the request is processed (**Figure 5.85**). Tap the X to cancel.

Figure 5.85 As the request is made, your location is shown on a map.

4. Once a car is confirmed, a map is displayed so you can watch the progress of the car coming to get you (**Figure 5.86**). Scroll down and you'll see the name of the driver, the kind of car they are driving, and their license plate number.

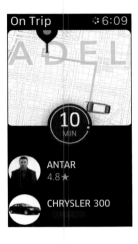

Figure 5.86 Once a car is assigned, the driver's name and the make and model of the car are displayed.

When the car is close to arriving, you'll be notified on your watch (and you'll also receive a text message, though that is part of the Uber service, not the Apple Watch app).

Get in the car, tell the driver where you want to go, and off you go.

Finding things to do

While Mary is on the road, she sometimes finds herself with some unscheduled time that she needs to fill. An hour here, an hour there. Combine this need with Apple Watch's knowledge of where she is and glanceable information, and she has the perfect job for the TripAdvisor Watch app (free, http://apple.co/1BqKDqi).

When you launch the TripAdvisor app on your watch (after installing it on your iPhone), it'll get your current location and present you with four options: Saved Places (saved from your iPhone or the watch), Restaurants, Things to Do, and Hotels (**Figure 5.87**).

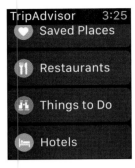

Figure 5.87 The TripAdvisor app lists things to do based on your current location.

Tap on any option other than Saved Places and the app will show you a list of those things nearby (**Figure 5.88**). Tap on one to get more information, including a phone number, a map (which you can tap on to get walking/driving directions from the Maps app), and reviews from other tourists. You can also add any of these places to your Saved Places on the watch by tapping the Save button in the details screen.

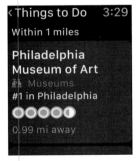

Figure 5.88 The Things to Do section lists attractions with ratings and how far they are from you.

Reminders

While you're on the go, whether you're traveling or just running an errand, sometimes a task that you need to do just pops into your head. You can use your Apple Watch to add those tasks to your Reminders list on your iPhone.

To create reminders on your Apple Watch:

1. Activate Siri by holding the Digital Crown in.

2. Say, "Remind me to pick up milk."

3. Siri will think for a moment and then show you the reminder she thinks you want to create (**Figure 5.89**). Tap OK to add it to your reminders.

Figure 5.89 Use Siri to add a reminder to your list. Don't forget the milk!

All reminders created on your Apple Watch will be added to your default Reminders list, which can be associated with any of the accounts (iCloud, Exchange) on your iPhone. To see what your default Reminders list is, tap Settings on your iPhone and then tap Reminders (**Figure 5.90**).

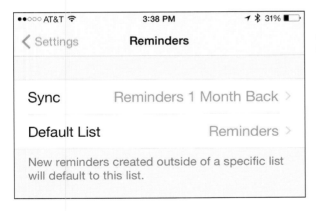

Figure 5.90 Any Reminders created on the watch will be added to your default reminders list.

The default list is shown. To change the default, tap on Default List (**Figure 5.91**). Any accounts that support reminders (or tasks as they are known in Exchange) will be listed. Tap to change your default.

You can also set due times/dates for reminders. Activate Siri and say something like, "Remind me to take out the trash in 10 minutes" and Siri will create a reminder with a due time of 10 minutes from the current time.

In 10 minutes you'll get a notification on your watch or phone that it is time to take out the trash.

If you use iCloud as your default list, you can also have *geofenced* reminders. These are reminders that have notifications triggered by you arriving or leaving a certain location. For example, you could activate Siri and say, "Remind me to take out the trash when I get home." Siri will ask you to confirm which address is your home address (**Figure 5.92**). Tap on the correct address and when you get home you'll find a notification reminding you to take out the trash.

Figure 5.92 If your Reminders list supports location-based reminders you can say, "Remind me to do something when I get home." If your home address isn't set, Siri will give you some options based on your contact.

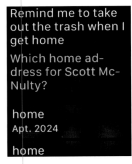

Reminders with due dates cause a notification to appear on your watch (**Figure 5.93**). Once you've completed the task, tap Completed and it'll be marked as complete on your Reminders list, no matter whether it is on iCloud or Exchange. If you need a little more time to complete the task, tap Snooze and you'll be reminded again in 10 minutes.

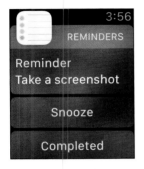

Figure 5.93 You can complete a reminder from its notification.

▶ **NOTE** There's no way to see your entire Reminders list on the Apple Watch. To do that you'll need to open the Reminders app on your iPhone or look at your tasks in your Exchange client of choice.

Evernote

Mary organizes her day in Evernote, and it's on all her devices. She puts her travel itineraries, notes, memos, and even pictures into Evernote. If she's on her computer, her iPhone, or her iPad, Evernote is always there for her.

Not too surprisingly, Evernote is on Mary's Apple Watch as well. It allows her to quickly access her notes without having to take her phone out of her pocket. She can even dictate a quick note and then come back to it on her Mac.

Since the Evernote Watch app is a companion app to the iPhone app, you don't need to log in. As long as you're logged into Evernote on your phone, launching the watch app (by pressing the Digital Crown until you're on the Home screen and then tapping the Evernote icon) will present you with a couple of buttons and some selected notes (**Figure 5.94**).

Figure 5.94 The Ever-
note Watch app gives
you access to your
notes on your wrist.

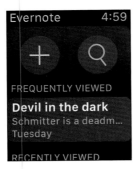

Tap the + button to add a new note to your Evernote notebook. Dictate
your note and then tap the Done button. A preview of your note appears,
along with a reminder icon and the Save button (**Figure 5.95**). To add a
reminder to the note, tap the Reminder button and specify when you want
to be reminded (**Figure 5.96**). Tap Save and the note will be saved to your
Evernote account.

Figure 5.95 Dictate notes
using Siri and save them to
Evernote.

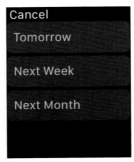

Figure 5.96 Set a reminder
on a note.

Creating notes is great, but the real power in Evernote is the accumulation
of your own knowledge that has been entered into it. The Evernote Watch
app displays your Recently Created, Frequently Viewed, and Recently
Viewed notes on the main screen. Use the Digital Crown to scroll through
the list. Tap on a note to read the whole thing on your watch (**Figure 5.97**).
Tap the upper-left corner to return to the list.

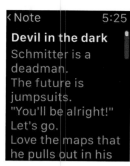

Figure 5.97 Read the full text of your notes.

If you've used Evernote for any length of time you'll have a lot of notes, more than could fit on the main screen. Tap the magnifying glass icon to search through all your notes.

The Search interface will show you a few of your frequently used tags and a dictation button (**Figure 5.98**). Tap one of the tags to see all the notes with that tag, or tap the dictation button to say a search phrase. Tap Done and all the matching notes will be displayed.

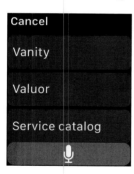

Figure 5.98 You can even search Evernote on your watch.

CHAPTER 6

Troubleshooting

Apple Watch is a version 1.0 product—Apple's first try at this. Given how new the device is, and how much functionality it offers, you can expect to run into some issues now and again. This chapter will show you have to force-quit an app, reboot your Apple Watch (even when it doesn't want to), unpair your watch from your iPhone, and restore your watch from a backup.

Force-Quit an App

If an app becomes unresponsive and tapping doesn't do anything, you can force it to quit. Force-quitting ends any processes that the app is running on the watch, including the one that has it hung up.

To force-quit an app:

1. With the app running, press and hold in the Side button until the shut-down screen appears (**Figure 6.1**).

Figure 6.1 Start with the basics: turn off your watch and turn it back on again.

2. Let go of the Side button and then press and hold it again. The display will flash onto the app and then very quickly show the clock face. That app has been quit.

    Try to relaunch the app and see if the behavior continues. If it does, you'll probably need to reinstall the app.

Reinstall an App

Sometimes you have to reinstall an app to make it work. This includes deleting it from the watch and reinstalling it via the Apple Watch app:

1. Press the Digital Crown until you're on the Home screen.

2. Press your finger against the display until the icons wiggle and an X appears in the corner of each icon (**Figure 6.2**).

Figure 6.2 Tap on the X to uninstall an app on your watch.

3. Tap the X on the app you want to delete.

4. When the confirmation appears, tap Delete App (**Figure 6.3**).

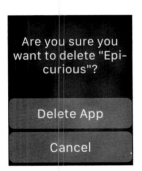

Figure 6.3 Tap Delete App to remove it.

5. Launch the Apple Watch app on your iPhone and find the app's name in the list.

6. Tap on the app name and then toggle on "Show App on Apple Watch."

7. The app is reinstalled, and then you can launch it on the watch once more.

Force-Restart the Watch

If the entire watch becomes unresponsive—tapping does nothing, and neither does pressing any of the buttons—it's time to force-restart the watch. None of your data will be lost, but the watch will reboot so you won't be able to use it for a few moments as it restarts.

To force-restart your watch, press in and hold both the Digital Crown and the Side button for about 10 seconds. Keep holding them both in until you see the Apple logo on the display. Once the Apple logo appears, you can let go of the buttons and allow the watch to reboot. It should work normally now.

> ► **TIP** If you continue to have issues with your watch becoming non-responsive, be sure to either call Apple or make an appointment at the nearest Genius Bar.

Unpair the Watch

Your Apple Watch must be paired with an iPhone to take full advantage of all it has to offer. There may come a time when you need to unpair the two devices. Perhaps you're selling your iPhone but you're holding onto the watch.

When you unpair an Apple Watch from its iPhone, all the content and settings on the watch are completely erased. Keep this in mind before you unpair your watch.

There are two ways to unpair a watch: via the Apple Watch app or on the watch itself. The preferred way to do it is via the iPhone app because whenever you unpair a watch using that method a backup of the watch is created (see the next section on how to restore a watch from a backup).

To unpair via the iPhone:

1. Launch the Apple Watch app and tap Apple Watch in the My Watch section.

2. Tap the red Unpair Apple Watch (**Figure 6.4**).

3. Tap Confirm. Your Apple Watch is backed up and then unpaired from the phone. The watch will reboot and then display the pairing pattern (see Chapter 1). It is ready to re-pair.

Figure 6.4 Tap Unpair Apple Watch on the Apple Watch app to decouple this phone from the listed watch.

To unpair from the watch you have to reset it to factory settings. This erases all the content on the watch, but unlike the previous method, no backup is made before it is erased.

To reset your watch (and unpair it) on the watch:

1. Press the Digital Crown until you're on the Home screen. Tap the Settings icon.

2. Tap General and scroll to the bottom where you will find Reset (**Figure 6.5**).

Figure 6.5 Under Settings > General you'll find Reset, which erases your watch and returns it to factory defaults.

3. Tap "Erase All Content and Settings."

4. Enter your passcode and your watch resets itself. Everything is erased, and the watch reboots into re-pairing mode.

Restore from Backup

To restore a watch from a backup, you need to pair it with an iPhone. Your watch is periodically backed up to the paired iPhone, so even if you unpaired the watch by erasing everything on it, chances are there's a backup to restore from.

Watch backups include

- General settings
- Language and Timezone
- Mail, Calendar, Stocks, and Weather settings
- App data
- Health and Fitness data

The Apple Watch's passcode, Apple Pay settings, and playlist/photos synced to the device are not included in the backup.

To restore your Apple Watch:

1. Launch the Apple Watch app on the iPhone you want to pair the watch to.

2. Tap Start Pairing and follow the directions on the iPhone.

3. You'll have the option to set up the watch as new or from a restore (**Figure 6.6**). Tap "Restore from Backup."

4. Choose a restore from the list (**Figure 6.7**). Each restore lists what kind of watch it is from and the date of the restore.

5. Complete the pairing process. Your iPhone will sync the restore to your Apple Watch and then you'll be able to use the device as if nothing happened.

Figure 6.6 Tap "Restore from Backup" to restore this watch from a backup.

Figure 6.7 Select the proper backup from the list.

Update the Watch

Apple Watch has an operating system that powers everything it does. From time to time, Apple will release an update to that operating system that will need to be installed on your watch.

A couple of things to know about installing updates on your watch:

- The paired iPhone needs to be connected to a Wi-Fi network to download the update.
- Your Apple Watch must have at least 50 percent battery power and be charging in order for the update to install.

The Apple Watch app will notify you that new software for the watch is available (**Figure 6.8**). Here's how to install it:

Figure 6.8 The Apple Watch app displays an alert when an update is available for Apple Watch.

1. Launch the Apple Watch app and you'll notice an alert in the General settings (**Figure 6.9**).

2. Tap General and you'll see another alert on the Software Update menu (**Figure 6.10**).

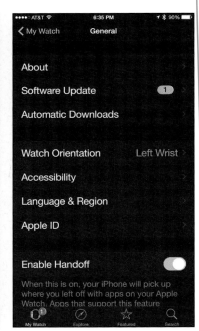

Figure 6.9 The General settings also have an alert, just to make sure you don't miss the update.

Figure 6.10 The Software Update menu lets you know one update is available.

3. Tap Software Update and you'll see some details about the available update (**Figure 6.11**). Tapping Learn More will tell you about the features and bug fixes included in the update.

4. Tap "Download and Install" and you'll be asked for your iPhone passcode (**Figure 6.12**). Enter it and tap Done.

Figure 6.11 Some details about the update, including the version number and a high-level description.

Figure 6.12 Enter your iPhone passcode to download the update.

5. Accept the terms and conditions by tapping Agree (**Figure 6.13**).

6. As the update downloads to your iPhone, the progress and time remaining is displayed (**Figure 6.14**). You can leave the Apple Watch app at this time and the download will continue in the background.

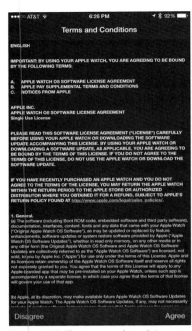

Figure 6.13 The terms and conditions are lengthy, but you can read them if you like.

Figure 6.14 Download times will vary, depending on network speeds.

7. Once the download is complete, the update is prepared for your watch (**Figure 6.15**). At this point, make sure that your watch is on the charger and that the iPhone is near it.

8. Your Apple Watch will warn you that an update is going to be installed (**Figure 6.16**).

   After several minutes your Apple Watch will reboot and the software update will be complete.

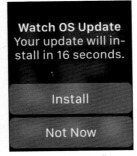

Figure 6.15 The iPhone prepares the update for the watch, just like a good friend should.

Figure 6.16 Tap Install to go ahead with the update or tap Not Now to delay it.

Index

M